BUILDING BUSINESS
God's Way

Published by ADAPT Publishing

Rancho Santa Margarita, Orange County, California

Edited and designed by Vicki Ramírez Fraga

Printed in the United States of America

ISBN: 979-8-9998062-4-6

Thomas Santos

BUILDING BUSINESS God's Way

12 BIBLICAL PRINCIPLES FOR BUILDING WHAT ENDURES

ADAPT Publishing

CONTENT

01

True success isn't measured by profit or recognition, but by faithfulness when no one is watching.

INTEGRITY AND HONESTY

The foundation of lasting influence.

Biblical integrity and honesty are essential for living in a way that truly reflects God's Word. They shape how we think, speak, and act—both in our personal lives and in the work we do every day.

Integrity means choosing to do what is right even when no one else is watching. It is about living with consistency, where our actions match our values, and where our character remains the same in public and in private. A person of integrity can be trusted because their words and actions align.

Honesty, closely tied to integrity, calls us to be truthful in every situation. It means dealing with others openly and fairly, without deceit, manipulation, or hidden motives. Together, integrity and honesty form the foundation of a life—and a business—that honors God and earns the trust of others.

BIBLICAL FOUNDATION

Proverbs 11:1

"THE LORD DETESTS DISHONEST SCALES, BUT ACCURATE WEIGHTS FIND FAVOR WITH HIM."

This verse teaches the importance God places on fairness and honesty in the way we do business. It clearly shows that integrity matters to Him and that dishonest practices are not pleasing in His sight. In a business context, it calls us to deal openly and fairly, ensuring that every transaction is transparent, ethical, and guided by a desire to honor God rather than gain an unfair advantage.

Colossians 3:23-24:

"WHATEVER YOU DO, WORK AT IT WITH ALL YOUR HEART, AS WORKING FOR THE LORD, NOT FOR HUMAN MASTERS, SINCE YOU KNOW THAT YOU WILL RECEIVE AN INHERITANCE FROM THE LORD AS A REWARD. IT IS THE LORD CHRIST YOU ARE SERVING."

This passage ecourages us to carry out our work with dedication and sincerity, viewing what we do as service to God rather than only to human employers. In a business setting, it calls us to give our best effort and to uphold high ethical standards, knowing that integrity, diligence, and faithfulness are ultimately seen and rewarded by God.

Proverbs 16:11:

"HONEST SCALES AND BALANCES BELONG TO THE LORD; ALL THE WEIGHTS IN THE BAG ARE OF HIS MAKING."

This scripture highlights that fairness and honesty in business are not simply human ideas, but principles established by God Himself. It underscores that ethical business practices align with God's order and invite His favor, calling us to uphold integrity in every transaction and decision.

Taken together, biblical instruction on integrity and honesty points to a life marked by ***truthfulness, fairness,*** and ***ethical conduct*** in every area—including business. These values ***honor God*** and, at the same time, ***help build trust and credibility*** in professional relationships. When business practices are shaped by these principles, they not only ***reflect faithfulness to God*** but also ***lay a strong foundation*** for work that is sustainable, meaningful, and lasting.

THE FRUIT VENDOR'S CHOICE

John was a Christian fruit vendor in a bustling market known for his fresh produce and warm smile. His stall was always busy, attracting both loyal and new customers. Yet, competition was fierce, and many vendors resorted to dishonest tactics—using faulty scales or misleading prices—to increase profits.

One day, a fellow vendor offered John a tempting idea.

"John," he said, "if you tweak your scales just a little, you can make a lot more money. Everyone else is doing it."

John's mind immediately went to Proverbs 11:1: "The LORD detests dishonest scales, but accurate weights find favor with Him." He knew he could not compromise his faith for quick gain. Guided by Colossians 3:23–24, he worked as if serving the Lord Himself, determined to honor God in every sale.

Though his honesty seemed costly at first, John's faithfulness brought long-term reward. Customers trusted him. His business grew—not through deceit, but through genuine relationships and divine favor. His example inspired other vendors to follow, transforming the marketplace into a community marked by fairness and integrity.

WISDOM TO BUILD ON

Integrity builds trust.

Trust strengthens influence.

Influence advances the Kingdom.

Honesty today plants the seeds of tomorrow's credibility.

BLUEPRINT FOR TODAY

Be transparent in every transaction, faithful in every promise, and truthful in every word. Let your work be worship, not manipulation.

Ask God to help you see where compromise has tried to enter your heart and to renew in you a spirit of integrity that honors Him in all you do.

BUILD YOUR BLUEPRINT

Honest Self-Assessment

Integrity begins with an honest look at ourselves.

Before we can build a culture of integrity in our business or leadership, we must first examine our own hearts. Scripture reminds us that God values truth not only in our actions, but also in the inner person.

Take a moment to reflect carefully and answer honestly.

> WHERE HAVE YOU FELT PRESSURE TO COMPROMISE INTEGRITY IN YOUR WORK OR LEADERSHIP?

> ARE THERE AREAS WHERE YOU HAVE ALLOWED "SMALL COMPROMISES" BECAUSE THEY SEEMED HARMLESS OR NORMAL IN YOUR INDUSTRY?

> WHERE COULD GREATER TRANSPARENCY STRENGTHEN TRUST IN YOUR LEADERSHIP OR ORGANIZATION?

Reflection Before God

Integrity is not merely a business principle — it is an act of worship.

When we work honestly, we acknowledge that our true Master is the Lord. As Colossians 3:23–24 reminds us, our work is ultimately done for Him.

Take a few moments to reflect prayerfully.

> WHAT PART OF THIS CHAPTER SPOKE MOST STRONGLY TO YOU? WHY?

____

____

____

____

____

____

> WHAT SITUATION IN YOUR LEADERSHIP CURRENTLY REQUIRES INTEGRITY AND COURAGE?

____

____

____

____

____

____

> WRITE A SHORT PRAYER ASK GOD TO SHAPE YOUR CHARACTER SO THAT YOUR WORK CONSISTENTLY REFLECTS HIS TRUTH.

____

____

____

____

____

____

____

Strategic Implementation

Integrity grows when it moves from conviction to action.

Think about specific ways you can strengthen honesty and transparency in your leadership, business practices, or team culture.

> ONE AREA WHERE I WILL STRENGTHEN INTEGRITY IMMEDIATELY:

____

____

____

____

____

> A POLICY, HABIT, OR PRACTICE THAT WOULD ENCOURAGE HONESTY IN MY ORGANIZATION:

____

____

____

____

____

> A SITUATION WHERE I NEED TO CORRECT SOMETHING THAT HAS NOT BEEN FULLY HONEST OR TRANSPARENT:

____

____

____

____

> A STEP I CAN TAKE THIS WEEK TO MODEL INTEGRITY FOR MY TEAM:

____

____

____

____

____

Growth and Accountability

Integrity grows through consistent choices ad intentional progress. Consider what you want to see developing in your leadership over time as you apply this principle.

> WHO COULD HELP HOLD YOU ACCOUNTABLE AS YOU GROW IN THIS AREA?

___

Define Your Growth Milestones

> IN THE NEXT 30 DAYS . TARGET DATE:________________________
>
> A SMALL BUT MEANINGFUL STEP TOWARD GREATER INTEGRITY:

___

___

___

> IN THE NEXT 90 DAYS. TARGET DATE:________________________

A VISIBLE CHANGE IN YOUR LEADERSHIP OR BUSINESS PRACTICES:

___

___

___

___

> IN THE NEXT 6 MONTHS. TARGET DATE:________________________
>
> A HABIT OR CULTURE YOU WANT TO SEE DEVELOPING IN YOUR ORGANIZATION:

___

___

___

___

> IN THE NEXT YEAR. TARGET DATE:________________________
>
> THE KIND OF LEADER YOU HOPE TO BECOME AS INTEGRITY DEEPENS IN YOUR LIFE:

___

___

___

Anticipating Challenges

> What pressures or situations might make it difficult to live out this principle?

> How will you respond if those challenges arise?

Evidence of Growth

> What signs would show that integrity is becoming stronger in your leadership and organization?

Reflection and Learning

After some time has passed, return to this page and reflect on what you experienced as you applied this principle.

> WHAT WENT WELL AS YOU PRACTICED THIS PRINCIPLE?

> WHAT DID YOU LEARN ABOUT YOUR LEADERSHIP OR CHARACTER?

> WHAT STILL NEEDS IMPROVEMENT OR DEEPER ATTENTION?

> WHAT WILL BE YOUR NEXT STEP FOR CONTINUED GROWTH?

Biblical Portrait

Joseph

Integrity When No One Is Watching

Sold into slavery by his own brothers, JOSEPH found himself far from home and serving in the house of Potiphar, an officer of Pharaoh. Yet even in this difficult position, Joseph chose to work faithfully. His diligence and honesty soon earned the complete trust of his master. Scripture tells us that Potiphar placed everything he owned under Joseph's care (Genesis 39:4–6).

But Joseph's greatest test came when no one else was watching.

Potiphar's wife repeatedly tried to seduce him. Joseph could have justified compromise. He was far from home, living as a slave, and the situation seemed hidden from others. Yet Joseph understood that integrity is ultimately lived before God.

His response reveals the foundation of his character:
"How then could I do this great evil and sin against God?" (Genesis 39:9).

Joseph refused the temptation, even though it cost him dearly. Potiphar's wife falsely accused him, and he was thrown into prison.

Integrity did not immediately reward him. But it preserved something far greater—his character and his relationship with God.

Years later, that same integrity prepared Joseph for leadership over all Egypt. When Pharaoh needed a trustworthy man to oversee the nation during famine, Joseph was ready.

His rise to power was not built on ambition or manipulation, but on proven character.

Joseph's story reminds us that integrity is often tested when compromise seems easy and hidden. Those who remain faithful in those moments build a foundation that God can trust with greater responsibility.

02

Everything we have—our time, talents, and resources—belongs to Him. We are caretakers, not owners, called to invest what He entrusts to us for His glory and the good of others.

STEWARDSHIP

Managing God's gifts with wisdom and purpose.

Biblical stewardship means living and working with the awareness that everything we possess ultimately belongs to God. In business, it calls for ethical management, accountability, and long-term vision rather than short-term gain. True stewards act with integrity and creativity, using their resources to serve others and honor the One who entrusted those resources to them.

When we understand that our success, skills, and opportunities are divine assignments, every decision becomes an act of worship. Stewardship is not about holding on—it's about multiplying what God has given for His Kingdom's impact.

BIBLICAL FOUNDATION

Matthew 25:14–30

THE PARABLE OF THE TALENTS

In this parable, Jesus tells the story of a master who, before leaving on a journey, entrusts his servants with different amounts of money. Each servant is given responsibility—not equally, but intentionally. When the master returns, he doesn't ask how much they were given; he asks what they did with it. Those who invested what they had and allowed it to grow are commended for their faithfulness. But the servant who hid his portion out of fear is corrected—not for losing anything, but for doing nothing.

The lesson is clear and challenging: what God entrusts to us is meant to be used, not buried. Faithfulness often requires courage, initiative, and trust. This passage invites us to step forward with what we've been given, to act wisely and creatively, and to resist the temptation to play it safe when growth and fruitfulness are possible.

1 Peter 4:10

"AS EACH HAS RECEIVED A GIFT, USE IT TO SERVE ONE ANOTHER, AS GOOD STEWARDS OF GOD'S VARIED GRACE."

This verse reminds us that no one is empty-handed. Each person has been entrusted with unique abilities, experiences, and opportunities—not for personal gain alone, but for the benefit of others. When we recognize our work and skills as gifts from God, stewardship becomes an act of service. In a business setting, this means using what we know, what we have, and what we build to strengthen others, encourage collaboration, and contribute to something greater than ourselves.

Colossians 3:23–24

"WHATEVER YOU DO, WORK HEARTILY, AS FOR THE LORD AND NOT FOR MEN, KNOWING THAT FROM THE LORD YOU WILL RECEIVE THE INHERITANCE AS YOUR REWARD. YOU ARE SERVING THE LORD CHRIST."

Here, Scripture shifts our focus from outcomes to motives. Our work is not merely a transaction or a means to recognition—it is an offering. When we work with sincerity, excellence, and integrity, we reflect who we ultimately serve. This perspective transforms everyday tasks into acts of worship and anchors ethical business practices in a deeper accountability, one that goes beyond human approval and rests in faithfulness to God.

Taken together, these principles paint a clear picture of biblical stewardship in the business world. It is the careful and intentional management of what God has entrusted to us—our time, talents, relationships, and resources. It calls us to invest wisely, act ethically, and work collaboratively, always remembering that our efforts are meant to serve others and honor God. When business is approached this way, it becomes not only productive, but purposeful—capable of creating lasting impact and sustainable good.

THE FAITHFUL ENTREPRENEUR

In the bustling city of Nairobi, a Christian entrepreneur named David built a thriving tech startup. He often said that his business was not his own—it belonged to God. This conviction shaped every aspect of his leadership.

Inspired by the Parable of the Talents in Matthew 25:14–30, David saw his resources as opportunities to multiply God's blessings. He invested in training programs for his employees, encouraging innovation and calculated risk-taking. Under his stewardship, his company developed groundbreaking software that brought both success and respect.

But David's vision extended beyond profit. Guided by 1 Peter 4:10, he believed his business existed to serve others. He launched community initiatives that offered free tech education to underprivileged youth, opening doors for hundreds of young people. His company became known not only for its innovation but for its generosity and compassion.

Motivated by Colossians 3:23–24, David reminded his team often: "We don't work for clients; we work for Christ." This mindset created a culture of integrity and diligence. His company flourished—not just financially, but as a testimony of what happens when stewardship is lived out with faith and purpose.

WISDOM TO BUILD ON

Faithful stewardship multiplies what He entrusts.

Serving others is at the heart of godly leadership.

Eternal impact outweighs temporary success.

Everything we manage belongs to God.

BLUEPRINT FOR TODAY

Work with the awareness that your resources, influence, and skills are divine assignments. Use them with wisdom, creativity, and compassion.

Ask God to help you recognize where you have buried your talents—and to give you courage to invest them boldly for His glory and the good of others.

BUILD YOUR BLUEPRINT

Honest Self-Assessment

Stewardship begins with recognizing that everything we manage ultimately belongs to God.

Our businesses, opportunities, resources, and influence are not truly ours—they are entrusted to us for a time. Scripture reminds us that faithful stewardship is measured not by ownership, but by responsibility.

Take a moment to reflect honestly about how you manage what has been entrusted to you.

> WHERE DO YOU SEE THE GREATEST RESPONSIBILITY GOD HAS ENTRUSTED TO YOU IN YOUR LEADERSHIP OR BUSINESS?

____

____

____

____

> ARE THERE AREAS WHERE YOU HAVE TREATED RESOURCES AS IF THEY BELONGED TO YOU RATHER THAN TO GOD?

____

____

____

____

> WHERE COULD GREATER FAITHFULNESS OR INTENTIONALITY IMPROVE THE WAY YOU MANAGE PEOPLE, FINANCES, OR OPPORTUNITIES?

____

____

____

____

____

Reflection Before God

Stewardship is ultimately a spiritual responsibility. God entrusts resources, opportunities, and influence to His people so they may be used for purposes that honor Him.

Jesus taught that faithfulness in small things prepares us for greater responsibility.

Take time to reflect prayerfully.

> What part of this chapter challenged your thinking about stewardship the most? Why?

____

____

____

____

> In what area of your leadership do you feel God calling you to greater faithfulness?

____

____

____

____

> Write a short prayer. Ask God to help you manage what He has entrusted to you with wisdom, humility, and faithfulness.

____

____

____

____

____

____

____

____

____

Strategic Implementation

Stewardship becomes visible through daily decisions.

Faithful leaders intentionally manage resources, people, and opportunities in ways that reflect God's priorities.

> ONE AREA WHERE I WILL BECOME A MORE FAITHFUL STEWARD IMMEDIATELY:

____

____

____

____

____

> A PRACTICAL STEP I CAN TAKE TO IMPROVE HOW I MANAGE RESOURCES IN MY LEADERSHIP OR ORGANIZATION:

____

____

____

____

____

> ONE WAY I CAN BETTER CARE FOR THE PEOPLE GOD HAS ENTRUSTED TO ME:

____

____

____

____

____

> A HABIT I CAN BEGIN THIS WEEK TO PRACTICE RESPONSIBLE STEWARDSHIP:

____

____

____

____

Growth and Accountability

Faithful stewardship develops over time through consistent choices and intentional growth.

> WHO COULD HELP HOLD YOU ACCOUNTABLE AS YOU GROW IN THIS AREA?

____

Define Your Growth Milestones

> IN THE NEXT 30 DAYS. TARGET DATE: ________________________
> A SMALL BUT MEANINGFUL STEP TOWARD MORE FAITHFUL STEWARDSHIP:

____

____

____

> IN THE NEXT 90 DAYS. TARGET DATE: ________________________
> A VISIBLE IMPROVEMENT IN HOW YOU MANAGE RESOURCES OR RESPONSIBILITIES:

____

____

____

> IN THE NEXT 6 MONTHS. TARGET DATE: ________________________
> A SYSTEM, HABIT, OR CULTURE YOU WANT TO SEE DEVELOPING IN YOUR ORGANIZATION:

____

____

____

____

> IN THE NEXT YEAR. TARGET DATE: ________________________
> THE KIND OF STEWARD YOU HOPE TO BECOME AS THIS PRINCIPLE SHAPES YOUR LEADERSHIP:

____

____

____

____

Anticipating Challenges

> WHAT PRESSURES OR CIRCUMSTANCES MIGHT MAKE IT DIFFICULT TO PRACTICE FAITHFUL STEWARDSHIP?

> HOW WILL YOU RESPOND WHEN THOSE CHALLENGES ARISE?

Evidence of Growth

> WHAT SIGNS WOULD SHOW THAT STEWARDSHIP IS IMPROVING IN YOUR LEADERSHIP AND ORGANIZATION?

> WHAT VISIBLE OUTCOMES WOULD REFLECT GREATER FAITHFULNESS IN MANAGING WHAT GOD HAS ENTRUSTED TO YOU?

Reflection and Learning

After some time has passed, return to this page and reflect on what you experienced as you applied this principle.

> WHAT WENT WELL AS YOU PRACTICED STEWARDSHIP?

____

> WHAT DID YOU LEARN ABOUT YOUR LEADERSHIP OR DECISION-MAKING?

> WHAT STILL NEEDS IMPROVEMENT OR DEEPER ATTENTION?

> WHAT WILL BE YOUR NEXT STEP FOR CONTINUED GROWTH?

BIBLICAL PORTRAIT

FAITHFUL STEWARDS

THE PARABLE OF THE TALENTS

Jesus often taught about stewardship through stories, and one of the clearest appears in the Parable of the Talents in Matthew 25:14–30.

In the story, a master prepares to leave on a journey. Before departing, he entrusts portions of his wealth to three servants. One receives five talents, another two, and another one. Each servant receives responsibility according to his ability.

What matters most is that the resources do not belong to the servants. They belong to the master. The servants are simply stewards, responsible for managing what has been entrusted to them.

The first two servants immediately put the talents to work and double what they received. When the master returns, he praises them with the same words: "Well done, good and faithful servant. You were faithful over a few things; I will make you ruler over many things" (Matthew 25:21).

The third servant, however, hides his talent out of fear. Instead of using what was entrusted to him, he chooses to preserve it. When the master returns, this servant is rebuked—not for losing the talent, but for failing to act.

Jesus' message is clear: stewardship is not about ownership, but faithfulness.

God entrusts every leader with resources—time, opportunities, influence, and responsibility. Some may receive more and others less, but the measure of stewardship is never the amount entrusted. It is the faithfulness with which it is managed.

Faithful leaders recognize that everything they oversee ultimately belongs to God, and they seek to use those resources wisely until the day they give account to Him.

03

In God's Kingdom, greatness is measured not by how many serve you, but by how faithfully you serve others.

SERVANT LEADERSHIP

True leadership begins with servanthood.

Servant leadership is not weakness—it is strength under control. It reflects the very heart of Jesus, who led through humility, compassion, and sacrifice. In the workplace, servant leadership transforms authority into stewardship. It builds teams grounded in trust, empathy, and shared purpose.

A servant leader doesn't ask, "How can they help me?" but rather, "How can I help them flourish?" This mindset reshapes organizations into communities of collaboration and care, where every individual's growth contributes to the greater good.

BIBLICAL FOUNDATION

Mark 10:45

"FOR EVEN THE SON OF MAN DID NOT COME TO BE SERVED, BUT TO SERVE, AND TO GIVE HIS LIFE AS A RANSOM FOR MANY."

In this statement, Jesus redefines what true leadership looks like. Though He held all authority, He chose the path of service. His leadership was not built on position or power, but on sacrifice and love for others. In a business or organizational setting, this challenges leaders to look beyond titles and privileges and instead ask how their role can genuinely serve employees, customers, and the mission they've been entrusted with.

Philippians 2:3–4

"DO NOTHING OUT OF SELFISH AMBITION OR VAIN CONCEIT. RATHER, IN HUMILITY VALUE OTHERS ABOVE YOURSELVES, NOT LOOKING TO YOUR OWN INTERESTS BUT EACH OF YOU TO THE INTERESTS OF THE OTHERS."

These verses call leaders to a posture of humility—one that resists ego and competition in favor of care and consideration. Valuing others does not mean neglecting responsibility or vision; it means leading with awareness, empathy, and respect. In the workplace, this kind of leadership creates space for growth, encourages collaboration, and builds teams where people feel seen, supported, and motivated to give their best.

Matthew 23:11

"THE GREATEST AMONG YOU WILL BE YOUR SERVANT."

Here, Jesus presents a radical truth: greatness is measured not by how many people serve us, but by how many we serve well. In business, this shifts leadership from control to empowerment. A servant-leader seeks to remove obstacles, develop others, and create systems that allow people to flourish—understanding that real influence is earned through trust and care, not authority alone.

Together, these passages form a compelling vision of biblical servant leadership. They remind us that leadership is ultimately relational and sacrificial, shaped by example rather than command. When leaders prioritize the well-being of others, cultivate humility, and serve with intentionality, they foster environments marked by unity, purpose, and trust. In business, this approach not only strengthens culture but also leads to lasting impact—where people grow, teams thrive, and success is shared.

THE CEO WHO SERVED FIRST

In the heart of Silicon Valley, a tech startup named GoodTech gained attention not only for its innovation but for its leadership philosophy. Its CEO, Sarah Thompson, was a devout Christian who believed that true leadership meant serving others first.

Sarah implemented policies that prioritized her employees' well-being and growth. Training, mentorship, and flexible work-life balance were core to her vision. She frequently reminded her team of Mark 10:45: "For even the Son of Man did not come to be served, but to serve, and to give His life as a ransom for many."

Her approach changed the culture of the company. During the development of a community-based app designed to connect people with essential services, Sarah encouraged her team using Philippians 2:3–4, urging them to focus on the common good over personal recognition. The team responded with unity and creativity, producing a tool that improved healthcare and education access in multiple regions.

As Matthew 23:11 says, "The greatest among you will be your servant." Sarah lived that truth daily. Her example inspired loyalty, motivation, and excellence across her team. Under her leadership, GoodTech not only succeeded financially—it became a company known for compassion, purpose, and impact.

WISDOM TO BUILD ON

Servant leaders put people before position.

True authority is earned through humility.

Leadership is not about being first—it's about lifting others higher.

When you serve, you lead hearts, not just hands.

BLUEPRINT FOR TODAY

Lead with the heart of a servant. Listen before directing, give before expecting, and love before leading.

Ask God to help you see how you can serve those you lead today—whether in your business, your team, or your home—and let your leadership point others to Him.

BUILD YOUR BLUEPRINT

Honest Self-Assessment

Servant leadership begins with a different understanding of leadership itself.

In many environments, leadership is associated with authority, control, or personal advancement. Yet Scripture presents a different model—one in which leaders serve the people entrusted to them.

Jesus Himself taught that true greatness is found not in being served, but in serving others.

Take a moment to reflect honestly.

> WHEN YOU THINK ABOUT LEADERSHIP, DO YOU NATURALLY FOCUS MORE ON AUTHORITY OR ON SERVICE?

____

____

____

____

> IN WHAT AREAS OF YOUR LEADERSHIP MIGHT PRIDE, CONTROL, OR RECOGNITION BECOME MORE IMPORTANT THAN SERVING OTHERS?

____

____

____

____

> WHERE DO YOU SEE OPPORTUNITIES TO SERVE THE PEOPLE GOD HAS ENTRUSTED TO YOU MORE INTENTIONALLY?

____

____

____

____

____

Reflection Before God

Servant leadership begins in the heart. It grows when leaders recognize that their position is an opportunity to care for and develop others.

Jesus reminded His disciples that leadership in God's kingdom looks very different from leadership in the world.

Take time to reflect prayerfully.

> WHAT PART OF THIS CHAPTER MOST CHALLENGED YOUR UNDERSTANDING OF LEADERSHIP?

____

____

____

____

____

> IN WHAT AREA OF YOUR LEADERSHIP DO YOU FEEL GOD CALLING YOU TO BECOME MORE SERVANT-HEARTED?

____

____

____

____

____

> WRITE A SHORT PRAYER.
> ASK GOD TO HELP YOU LEAD WITH HUMILITY, COMPASSION, AND A GENUINE DESIRE TO SERVE OTHERS.

____

____

____

____

____

____

____

Strategic Implementation

Servant leadership becomes visible through daily attitudes and actions. Leaders who serve others intentionally create environments where people can grow, contribute, and thrive.

> ONE AREA WHERE I CAN PRACTICE SERVANT LEADERSHIP IMMEDIATELY:

> ONE PRACTICAL WAY I CAN SUPPORT OR DEVELOP SOMEONE ON MY TEAM:

> A STEP I CAN TAKE TO ENSURE THE PEOPLE I LEAD FEEL VALUED AND CARED FOR:

> ONE HABIT I CAN BEGIN THIS WEEK THAT REFLECTS A SERVANT LEADER'S MINDSET:

Growth and Accountability

Servant leadership develops over time through intentional choices and consistent humility.

> WHO COULD HELP HOLD YOU ACCOUNTABLE AS YOU GROW IN THIS AREA?

____

Define Your Growth Milestones

> IN THE NEXT 30 DAYS. TARGET DATE: ______________________
> A SMALL BUT MEANINGFUL STEP TOWARD SERVING OTHERS MORE INTENTIONALLY:

____

____

____

> IN THE NEXT 90 DAYS. TARGET DATE: ______________________
> A VISIBLE CHANGE IN HOW YOU SUPPORT, ENCOURAGE, OR DEVELOP THE PEOPLE YOU LEAD:

____

____

____

____

> IN THE NEXT 6 MONTHS. TARGET DATE: ______________________
> A HABIT OR LEADERSHIP CULTURE YOU WANT TO SEE DEVELOPING IN YOUR ORGANIZATION:

____

____

____

____

> IN THE NEXT YEAR. TARGET DATE: ______________________
> THE KIND OF SERVANT LEADER YOU HOPE TO BECOME AS HUMILITY GROWS IN YOUR LEADERSHIP:

____

____

____

Anticipating Challenges

> WHAT ATTITUDES OR PRESSURES MIGHT MAKE SERVANT LEADERSHIP DIFFICULT?

> HOW WILL YOU RESPOND WHEN THOSE CHALLENGES ARISE?

Evidence of Growth

> WHAT SIGNS WOULD SHOW THAT SERVANT LEADERSHIP IS BECOMING STRONGER IN YOUR LEADERSHIP?

> WHAT VISIBLE CHANGES WOULD REFLECT A HEALTHIER LEADERSHIP CULTURE IN YOUR ORGANIZATION?

Reflection and Learning

After some time has passed, return to this page and reflect on what you experienced as you applied this principle.

> WHAT WENT WELL AS YOU PRACTICED SERVANT LEADERSHIP?

> WHAT DID YOU LEARN ABOUT YOURSELF AS A LEADER?

> WHAT STILL NEEDS IMPROVEMENT OR DEEPER ATTENTION?

> WHAT WILL BE YOUR NEXT STEP FOR CONTINUED GROWTH?

Biblical Portrait

Jesus

The Servant King

JESUS provides the ultimate example of servant leadership.

Though He was the Son of God, Jesus did not lead through power or privilege. Instead, He consistently demonstrated humility and service toward others. One of the most striking moments of this appears in John 13, when Jesus washed the feet of His disciples.

In that culture, washing feet was the task of the lowest servant in a household. Yet Jesus, the Teacher and Lord, chose to kneel before His disciples and perform this act of service.

Afterward He explained the meaning of His actions: “If I then, your Lord and Teacher, have washed your feet, you also ought to wash one another’s feet” (John 13:14).

Jesus was showing them that leadership in God’s kingdom is not about status or authority, but about serving others.

Throughout His ministry, Jesus invested in people, taught them patiently, cared for their needs, and ultimately gave His life for them. His leadership was marked by sacrifice, compassion, and humility.

Servant leadership does not diminish authority—it strengthens it. When leaders genuinely serve those they lead, they build trust, loyalty, and influence.

Jesus reminds us that the greatest leaders are not those who seek to be served, but those who willingly serve others.

04

Effort without excuses and perseverance without pride reveal a heart that works for the Lord rather than for men.

HARD WORK AND DILIGENCE

Hard work honors God and diligence builds lasting success.

Hard work and diligence are not simply about productivity—they are expressions of faithfulness. God designed work as a means of purpose and worship. Every task, whether seen or unseen, becomes sacred when done wholeheartedly unto Him.

In business, diligence means consistency, excellence, and a refusal to give up when challenges arise. Hard work, rooted in humility, doesn't seek applause but impact. It is through persistence and integrity that God refines both our character and our calling.

BIBLICAL FOUNDATION

Colossians 3:23–24

"WHATEVER YOU DO, WORK HEARTILY, AS FOR THE LORD AND NOT FOR MEN, KNOWING THAT FROM THE LORD YOU WILL RECEIVE THE INHERITANCE AS YOUR REWARD. YOU ARE SERVING THE LORD CHRIST."

These verses elevate our view of work by anchoring it in purpose. Our daily tasks—whether visible or unseen—are not merely obligations but opportunities to serve God through faithfulness and excellence. When work is approached with this mindset, integrity becomes non-negotiable, motivation deepens, and excellence becomes an act of worship rather than a pursuit of recognition.

Proverbs 14:23

"IN ALL TOIL THERE IS PROFIT, BUT MERE TALK TENDS ONLY TO POVERTY."

This proverb draws a clear line between intention and action. While ideas, plans, and conversations have their place, Scripture reminds us that progress is ultimately born out of effort. Results come through showing up, working consistently, and following through. In the business world, this wisdom speaks directly to the value of disciplined labor—where commitment and perseverance, not just good intentions, lead to growth and stability.

Ecclesiastes 9:10

"WHATEVER YOUR HAND FINDS TO DO, DO IT WITH YOUR MIGHT, FOR THERE IS NO WORK OR THOUGHT OR KNOWLEDGE OR WISDOM IN SHEOL, TO WHICH YOU ARE GOING."

Ecclesiastes reminds us of the urgency and value of wholehearted effort. The opportunities we are given—to create, build, lead, and contribute—are not endless. This truth encourages us to engage fully in the work before us, applying our skills, energy, and wisdom with intention. In business, this translates into diligence, focus, and a refusal to settle for mediocrity when meaningful impact is possible.

Taken together, these Scriptures present a compelling vision of work rooted in diligence, purpose, and faithfulness. True success is not merely measured by profit or productivity, but by the integrity and commitment with which we labor. When hard work is embraced as a calling and effort is offered with sincerity, business becomes more than a pursuit of gain—it becomes a space for fulfillment, growth, and lasting significance, reflecting the values Scripture has taught all along.

THE RELENTLESS ENTREPRENEUR

John, a devout Christian and aspiring entrepreneur, found himself at a crossroads after graduating college. He had a brilliant idea but no funding or connections. Remembering Proverbs 14:23, he resolved that his strongest capital would be hard work.

From a small apartment, he poured long hours into refining his business plan and researching his market. His dedication spoke louder than any presentation. Eventually, a local investor noticed not just his idea but his diligence and integrity.

As his business began to grow, John embraced the truth of Colossians 3:23–24. Every decision, every deal, became an act of service to God. His work ethic created a culture of integrity and purpose—his employees caught his vision and his customers trusted his brand.

When challenges came, Ecclesiastes 9:10 echoed in his mind: "Whatever your hand finds to do, do it with your might." John persevered through late nights and setbacks, knowing that every opportunity was fleeting and precious. His consistency led to success—industry recognition, financial growth, and a legacy built on biblical diligence.

Through his story, John proved that the road to true prosperity is paved with faith, focus, and hard work that honors God above all else.

WISDOM TO BUILD ON

God blesses consistent effort more than fleeting inspiration.

Hard work is a form of worship.

Perseverance refines both character and calling.

Diligence turns vision into victory.

BLUEPRINT FOR TODAY

Approach today's work as sacred service. Refuse laziness, distraction, or half-hearted effort. Whatever your hands find to do, do it with all your might and all your heart.

Ask God to help you see your work through His eyes—to find joy in diligence and purpose in persistence, trusting that your labor in the Lord is never in vain.

BUILD YOUR BLUEPRINT

Honest Self-Assessment

Hard work and diligence are foundational to faithful leadership.

Scripture consistently teaches that diligence leads to growth, provision, and opportunity, while laziness leads to lack. Yet diligence is not only about working hard—it is about working faithfully, consistently, and with purpose.

Take a moment to reflect honestly.

> DO YOU TEND TO APPROACH YOUR WORK WITH CONSISTENCY AND DISCIPLINE, OR DO YOU STRUGGLE WITH PROCRASTINATION OR INCONSISTENCY?

____

____

____

____

____

> IN WHAT AREAS OF YOUR LEADERSHIP OR WORK COULD GREATER DILIGENCE IMPROVE RESULTS?

____

____

____

____

____

> ARE THERE RESPONSIBILITIES YOU HAVE BEEN AVOIDING OR DELAYING THAT REQUIRE FAITHFUL ATTENTION?

____

____

____

____

____

Reflection Before God

Diligence is not simply about productivity—it is an expression of faithfulness to God.

When we work with consistency and care, we reflect a heart that values what God has entrusted to us. Scripture reminds us that our work is ultimately done for Him.

Take time to reflect prayerfully.

> WHAT PART OF THIS CHAPTER MOST CHALLENGED YOUR VIEW OF WORK AND DILIGENCE?

____

____

____

____

____

> WHERE DO YOU FEEL GOD CALLING YOU TO GREATER DISCIPLINE OR CONSISTENCY?

____

____

____

____

____

> WRITE A SHORT PRAYER.
> ASK GOD TO STRENGTHEN YOUR DISCIPLINE AND HELP YOU WORK WITH FAITHFULNESS AND PERSEVERANCE.

____

____

____

____

____

____

____

Strategic Implementation

Diligence is built through consistent action. Leaders who practice diligence create stability, reliability, and momentum in their work and in their organizations.

> ONE AREA WHERE I WILL APPLY GREATER DILIGENCE IMMEDIATELY:

> A TASK OR RESPONSIBILITY I NEED TO ADDRESS WITH GREATER CONSISTENCY:

> A HABIT I CAN DEVELOP TO IMPROVE DISCIPLINE IN MY DAILY WORK:

> ONE STEP I CAN TAKE THIS WEEK TO WORK WITH GREATER FOCUS AND INTENTIONALITY:

Growth and Accountability

Diligence grows through consistent effort and intentional habits over time.

> WHO COULD HELP HOLD YOU ACCOUNTABLE AS YOU GROW IN THIS AREA?

____

Define Your Growth Milestones

> IN THE NEXT 30 DAYS. TARGET DATE: ______________________
> A SMALL BUT MEANINGFUL STEP TOWARD GREATER DILIGENCE:

____

____

____

> IN THE NEXT 90 DAYS. TARGET DATE: ______________________
> A VISIBLE IMPROVEMENT IN YOUR DISCIPLINE OR CONSISTENCY:

____

____

____

____

> IN THE NEXT 6 MONTHS. TARGET DATE: ______________________
> A HABIT OR SYSTEM YOU WANT TO SEE FIRMLY ESTABLISHED:

____

____

____

____

> IN THE NEXT YEAR. TARGET DATE: ______________________
> THE KIND OF WORKER AND LEADER YOU HOPE TO BECOME THROUGH DILIGENCE:

____

____

____

Anticipating Challenges

> WHAT DISTRACTIONS, HABITS, OR PRESSURES MIGHT HINDER YOUR DILIGENCE?

> HOW WILL YOU RESPOND WHEN THOSE CHALLENGES ARISE?

Evidence of Growth

> WHAT SIGNS WOULD SHOW THAT DILIGENCE IS INCREASING IN YOUR WORK AND LEADERSHIP?

> WHAT VISIBLE RESULTS WOULD REFLECT GREATER CONSISTENCY AND DISCIPLINE?

Reflection and Learning

After some time has passed, return to this page and reflect on what you experienced as you applied this principle.

> WHAT WENT WELL AS YOU PRACTICED DILIGENCE?

> WHAT DID YOU LEARN ABOUT YOUR WORK HABITS OR DISCIPLINE?

> WHAT DID YOU LEARN ABOUT YOUR WORK HABITS OR DISCIPLINE?

> WHAT WILL BE YOUR NEXT STEP FOR CONTINUED GROWTH?

Biblical Portrait

Ruth

Diligence that Leads to Provision

RUTH provides a beautiful example of diligence lived out with humility and faithfulness.

After losing her husband, Ruth chose to remain with Naomi and journey to Bethlehem, entering a land where she had no security or status. Rather than waiting for provision, Ruth took initiative. She went out to glean in the fields, gathering leftover grain behind the harvesters so that she and Naomi could survive.

Her work was not easy. It required long hours, physical effort, and persistence. Yet Ruth approached it with a willing and diligent spirit.

When Boaz, the owner of the field, noticed her, he asked about her. The report he received was telling: she had been working steadily from morning until evening, with only short rests (Ruth 2:7).

Her diligence did not go unnoticed.

Boaz not only allowed her to continue gleaning but showed her kindness and provision. Over time, Ruth's faithful work led to greater blessing, security, and ultimately restoration.

Ruth's story reminds us that diligence is often expressed in small, consistent acts of faithfulness. She did not begin with position or influence, but with willingness to work.

God used that diligence to open doors she could not have created on her own.

In leadership and business, the same principle remains true. Diligence may seem ordinary in the moment, but over time it builds opportunity, trust, and provision.

Faithful work, done consistently, becomes a pathway through which God brings growth and blessing.

05

When we give freely and cheerfully, we reflect the heart of our Father, who withholds nothing good from His children.

GENEROSITY AND GIVING

Generosity opens the door for God's abundance.

Biblical generosity is more than an act—it's a posture of the heart. It flows from recognizing that everything we have belongs to God, and we are called to be channels, not reservoirs, of His blessings.

In business, generosity is expressed through fairness, compassion, and responsible stewardship. It's found in how we treat employees, support communities, and share resources. When generosity defines a company's culture, it creates an atmosphere of trust and blessing that cannot be replicated by marketing or strategy alone.

BIBLICAL FOUNDATION

2 Corinthians 9:6–7

"REMEMBER THIS: WHOEVER SOWS SPARINGLY WILL ALSO REAP SPARINGLY, AND WHOEVER SOWS GENEROUSLY WILL ALSO REAP GENEROUSLY. EACH OF YOU SHOULD GIVE WHAT YOU HAVE DECIDED IN YOUR HEART TO GIVE, NOT RELUCTANTLY OR UNDER COMPULSION, FOR GOD LOVES A CHEERFUL GIVER."

Here, Scripture speaks not only to how much we give, but how we give. Generosity is meant to be intentional, willing, and rooted in the heart—not driven by pressure or appearances. Applied to business, this principle encourages thoughtful investment in employees, communities, and initiatives that bring genuine good. When giving flows from conviction rather than obligation, it cultivates trust, loyalty, and lasting impact.

Proverbs 11:25

"A GENEROUS PERSON WILL PROSPER; WHOEVER REFRESHES OTHERS WILL BE REFRESHED."

This proverb captures a timeless principle: generosity is never wasted. When we choose to give—our time, resources, encouragement, or opportunities—we participate in a cycle of renewal that blesses both the giver and the receiver. In a business setting, this truth invites leaders and organizations to look beyond short-term gain and invest in people, fairness, and support. Prosperity, according to Scripture, often flows through generosity, not away from it.

Luke 6:38

"GIVE, AND IT WILL BE GIVEN TO YOU. A GOOD MEASURE, PRESSED DOWN, SHAKEN TOGETHER AND RUNNING OVER, WILL BE POURED INTO YOUR LAP. FOR WITH THE MEASURE YOU USE, IT WILL BE MEASURED TO YOU."

Jesus describes generosity as an act that releases abundance. This is not a mechanical transaction, but a spiritual reality: open hands tend to receive more than clenched ones. In the workplace, generosity expressed through ethical practices, care for employees, and meaningful community engagement often returns in the form of stronger relationships, healthier culture, and sustained growth. Wholehearted giving creates momentum that extends far beyond the initial act.

Together, these passages reveal generosity as both a spiritual posture and a practical way of life. In business, generosity shapes how decisions are made, how people are valued, and how success is defined. Organizations that operate with open hearts and open hands often discover that generosity produces a ripple effect—cultivating goodwill, strengthening reputation, and fostering long-term fruitfulness. When giving becomes part of the culture, prosperity follows in ways that reach far beyond the bottom line.

THE BAKERY THAT BLESSED A CITY

In the bustling city of Atlanta, a Christian entrepreneur named Sarah Thompson owned a small bakery called Heavenly Delights. From the beginning, she viewed her business not as a means of profit, but as a ministry of provision.

Sarah began by donating a portion of her profits to local food banks and shelters. Inspired by Proverbs 11:25, she trusted that by refreshing others, she herself would be refreshed. Her customers noticed the warmth behind her mission. Soon, her bakery became a gathering place not just for pastries, but for purpose.

Guided by 2 Corinthians 9:6–7, Sarah encouraged her employees to give back as well—volunteering at community events, with paid time off for those who served. She also provided scholarships for team members pursuing education or personal growth. Her heart for giving created loyalty and joy among her staff, who saw themselves as partners in something bigger than business.

As the years passed, Luke 6:38 became her testimony: "A good measure, pressed down, shaken together, and running over." Her generosity returned in abundance—faithful customers, a thriving team, and opportunities to expand her reach.

Heavenly Delights became more than a bakery; it became a beacon of kindness in the city, proving that when we give from the heart, God multiplies far beyond what we could imagine.

WISDOM TO BUILD ON

A cheerful heart multiplies blessing in every direction.

Giving transforms both the giver and the receiver.

Generosity invites God's abundance.

When you refresh others, God refreshes you.

BLUEPRINT FOR TODAY

Look for ways to bless others through your work—employees, customers, or your community. Give joyfully and consistently, knowing that generosity reflects the very nature of God.

Ask God to help you see where He wants you to give more freely—of your time, resources, or encouragement—and trust that His return will overflow beyond measure.

BUILD YOUR BLUEPRINT

Honest Self-Assessment

Generosity begins with recognizing that everything we have ultimately comes from God.

In leadership and business, it is easy to focus on growth, accumulation, and security. Yet Scripture reminds us that we are not only called to manage resources, but also to give.

Generosity reveals what we truly trust.

Take a moment to reflect honestly.

> Do you tend to approach resources with an open hand or a protective mindset?

____

____

____

____

____

> In what areas do you find it difficult to give—time, money, attention, or opportunity?

____

____

____

____

____

> Where could greater generosity positively impact the people around you?

____

____

____

____

____

Reflection Before God

Generosity is not measured by the amount we give, but by the heart with which we give.

Jesus taught that giving reflects trust in God and love for others. When we give, we acknowledge that God is our provider.

Take time to reflect prayerfully.

> WHAT PART OF THIS CHAPTER MOST CHALLENGED YOUR PERSPECTIVE ON GIVING?

> WHERE DO YOU SENSE GOD INVITING YOU TO TRUST HIM MORE THROUGH GENEROSITY?

> WRITE A SHORT PRAYER.
> ASK GOD TO SHAPE YOUR HEART SO THAT GIVING BECOMES A JOYFUL AND NATURAL RESPONSE TO HIS PROVISION.

Strategic Implementation

Generosity becomes visible through intentional and consistent action. Leaders who give freely create environments of trust, care, and encouragement.

> ONE AREA WHERE I CAN PRACTICE GREATER GENEROSITY IMMEDIATELY:

> A WAY I CAN BLESS OR SUPPORT SOMEONE THIS WEEK:

> A PRACTICAL STEP I CAN TAKE TO MAKE GIVING A REGULAR PART OF MY LIFE OR LEADERSHIP:

> A HABIT I CAN BEGIN THIS WEEK THAT REFLECTS A MORE GENEROUS LIFESTYLE:

Growth and Accountability

Generosity grows as we practice it consistently over time.

> WHO COULD HELP HOLD YOU ACCOUNTABLE AS YOU GROW IN THIS AREA?

____

Define Your Growth Milestones

> IN THE NEXT 30 DAYS. TARGET DATE: ______________________
> A SMALL BUT MEANINGFUL ACT OF GENEROSITY:

____

____

____

> IN THE NEXT 90 DAYS. TARGET DATE: ______________________
> A VISIBLE CHANGE IN HOW YOU GIVE YOUR RESOURCES OR TIME:

____

____

____

____

> IN THE NEXT 6 MONTHS. TARGET DATE: ______________________
> A HABIT OR RHYTHM OF GIVING YOU WANT TO ESTABLISH:

____

____

____

____

> IN THE NEXT YEAR. TARGET DATE: ______________________
> THE KIND OF GIVER YOU HOPE TO BECOME AS GENEROSITY SHAPES YOUR LIFE:

____

____

____

____

Anticipating Challenges

> WHAT FEARS OR CONCERNS MIGHT MAKE GENEROSITY DIFFICULT?

> HOW WILL YOU RESPOND WHEN THOSE CHALLENGES ARISE?

Evidence of Growth

> WHAT SIGNS WOULD SHOW THAT GENEROSITY IS INCREASING IN YOUR LIFE AND LEADERSHIP?

> WHAT VISIBLE CHANGES WOULD REFLECT A CULTURE OF GIVING AROUND YOU?

Reflection and Learning

After some time has passed, return to this page and reflect on what you experienced as you applied this principle.

> WHAT WENT WELL AS YOU PRACTICED GENEROSITY?

> WHAT DID YOU LEARN ABOUT YOUR HEART OR YOUR TRUST IN GOD?

> WHAT STILL NEEDS IMPROVEMENT OR DEEPER ATTENTION?

> WHAT WILL BE YOUR NEXT STEP FOR CONTINUED GROWTH?

Biblical Portrait

The Widow

Generosity that Trusts God

Jesus once sat near the temple treasury watching people give their offerings (Mark 12:41–44). Many rich individuals contributed large amounts, giving out of their abundance.

Then A POOR WIDOW came and placed two small coins into the offering—an amount that seemed insignificant compared to the others.

Yet Jesus called His disciples and made a surprising statement. He told them that this widow had given more than all the others.

Why?

Because they gave out of their surplus, but she gave out of her poverty. She put in all she had to live on.

Her gift was small in value, but great in sacrifice.

The widow's generosity reveals a deeper truth: giving is not measured by the amount, but by the heart. She trusted God completely, even when her resources were limited.

Her act was not driven by obligation or recognition, but by faith.

In leadership and business, generosity often feels easier when there is abundance. But true generosity is revealed when giving requires trust.

The widow reminds us that generosity is not about how much we have, but about how much we are willing to trust God with what we have.

A generous heart reflects confidence in God's provision—and that kind of trust never goes unnoticed by Him.

06

A trustworthy person reflects the very nature of God—reliable, steadfast, and true.

TRUST-WORTHINESS AND FAITHFULNESS

Faithfulness in small things builds the foundation for greater things.

Trustworthiness and faithfulness are not only moral virtues; they are reflections of God's own character. He is faithful in every promise, unwavering in every word, and constant in every season. When we model His faithfulness in our business and relationships, we become living testimonies of His reliability.

In a world that often rewards shortcuts and compromise, being trustworthy sets believers apart. It creates stability in organizations, peace in partnerships, and influence that endures. Faithfulness is not just about doing what's right once—it's about doing what's right consistently, even when no one notices.

BIBLICAL FOUNDATION

Colossians 3:23–24

"WHATEVER YOU DO, WORK AT IT WITH ALL YOUR HEART, AS WORKING FOR THE LORD, NOT FOR HUMAN MASTERS, SINCE YOU KNOW THAT YOU WILL RECEIVE AN INHERITANCE FROM THE LORD AS A REWARD. IT IS THE LORD CHRIST YOU ARE SERVING."

These verses lift our understanding of work beyond obligation or recognition. When our efforts are offered sincerely and wholeheartedly, they become an expression of service to God Himself. In business, this perspective shapes a work ethic marked by excellence, accountability, and perseverance. It encourages people to act with integrity—not because they are being monitored, but because their work reflects whom they ultimately serve.

Proverbs 11:1

"A FALSE BALANCE IS AN ABOMINATION TO THE LORD, BUT A JUST WEIGHT IS HIS DELIGHT."

This proverb speaks directly to the heart of integrity. God cares deeply about honesty in everyday dealings—about accuracy, fairness, and transparency. In business terms, this means conducting transactions with truthfulness and refusing to cut corners, even when doing so might seem profitable in the short term. Trust is built when others know they are being treated fairly, and Scripture reminds us that such integrity is not only good practice—it delights the Lord.

Luke 16:10

"WHOEVER CAN BE TRUSTED WITH VERY LITTLE CAN ALSO BE TRUSTED WITH MUCH, AND WHOEVER IS DISHONEST WITH VERY LITTLE WILL ALSO BE DISHONEST WITH MUCH."

Jesus highlights a simple but profound principle: character is revealed in small things. Faithfulness in minor responsibilities reflects a heart that can be entrusted with greater ones. In the workplace, this means that attention to detail, honesty in routine tasks, and consistency in commitments matter more than we often realize. Trust grows when reliability is demonstrated day after day, even when no one seems to be watching.

Together, these passages form a strong foundation for understanding trustworthiness and faithfulness from a biblical perspective. They call us to live out our commitments with consistency, honesty, and care—both in visible decisions and quiet responsibilities. In business, these values cultivate credibility, strengthen relationships, and establish cultures where people can depend on one another. Over time, faithfulness proves to be one of the most valuable assets an organization can possess, leading to lasting success rooted in integrity.

THE BAKERY THAT CHOSE INTEGRITY

In the bustling city of Atlanta, John and Mary owned a small but thriving bakery called Heaven's Delight. Their pastries were known for their quality, but their reputation was built on something deeper—their unwavering honesty and faithfulness to God's principles.

One day, a major corporate client offered them a lucrative contract, on one condition: they had to lower their standards and use cheaper ingredients. It was a tempting offer that could have doubled their income. But John remembered Proverbs 11:1: "A false balance is an abomination to the LORD, but a just weight is His delight." He and Mary prayed, deciding that faithfulness mattered more than financial success.

They respectfully declined the offer. Word spread about their integrity, and customers began seeking them out for their honest practices and quality work. As business grew, John reflected on Luke 16:10: "Whoever can be trusted with very little can also be trusted with much." Their faithfulness in small things had led to greater trust, both from God and their community.

In time, Heaven's Delight became known not only for its pastries but for its principles. Every cake, loaf, and cookie became an offering of worship, done "as for the Lord," just as Colossians 3:23–24 declares. Their story became a living example that faithfulness in business invites both blessing and lasting influence.

WISDOM TO BUILD ON

God delights in integrity and consistency.

A trustworthy reputation is more valuable than wealth.

Faithfulness in small things prepares us for greater responsibility.

When you work for God, every task becomes sacred.

BLUEPRINT FOR TODAY

Be faithful in the small details of your work. Follow through on your word, honor your commitments, and choose integrity even when compromise seems easier.

Ask God to help you see the opportunities hidden in faithfulness—and to make your life a reflection of His unwavering trustworthiness.

BUILD YOUR BLUEPRINT

Honest Self-Assessment

Trustworthiness is built through consistent faithfulness over time.

In leadership and business, people rely on those who are dependable, honest, and consistent. Faithfulness is not proven in a single moment, but through daily choices that reflect integrity and responsibility.

Take a moment to reflect honestly.

> WOULD OTHERS DESCRIBE YOU AS CONSISTENT AND DEPENDABLE IN YOUR RESPONSIBILITIES?

____

____

____

____

____

____

> ARE THERE AREAS WHERE YOU HAVE BEEN INCONSISTENT, UNRELIABLE, OR SLOW TO FOLLOW THROUGH?

____

____

____

____

____

> WHERE COULD GREATER FAITHFULNESS STRENGTHEN TRUST IN YOUR LEADERSHIP OR RELATIONSHIPS?

____

____

____

____

____

Reflection Before God

Faithfulness is deeply connected to our relationship with God.

Scripture teaches that those who are faithful in small things will be entrusted with greater responsibility. God values consistency, reliability, and a heart that remains steady over time.

Take time to reflect prayerfully.

> WHAT PART OF THIS CHAPTER MOST CHALLENGED YOUR UNDERSTANDING OF FAITHFULNESS?

____

____

____

____

____

> IN WHAT AREA DO YOU FEEL GOD CALLING YOU TO GREATER CONSISTENCY AND TRUSTWORTHINESS?

____

____

____

____

____

> WRITE A SHORT PRAYER.
> ASK GOD TO STRENGTHEN YOUR FAITHFULNESS SO THAT YOUR LIFE REFLECTS RELIABILITY AND INTEGRITY IN EVERY AREA.

____

____

____

____

____

____

____

____

Strategic Implementation

Faithfulness becomes visible through consistent action and follow-through. Leaders who are trustworthy create stability, confidence, and long-term impact.

> One area where I will become more faithful immediately:

____

____

____

____

____

> A responsibility I need to handle with greater consistency or care:

____

____

____

____

____

> A practical step I can take to improve reliability in my leadership:

____

____

____

____

____

> One habit I can begin this week that reflects greater faithfulness:

____

____

____

____

____

Growth and Accountability

Faithfulness grows through steady commitment and intentional habits.

> WHO COULD HELP HOLD YOU ACCOUNTABLE AS YOU GROW IN THIS AREA?

____

Define Your Growth Milestones

> IN THE NEXT 30 DAYS. TARGET DATE: ______________________
>
> A SMALL BUT MEANINGFUL STEP TOWARD GREATER TRUSTWORTHINESS:

____

____

____

> IN THE NEXT 90 DAYS. TARGET DATE: ______________________
>
> A VISIBLE IMPROVEMENT IN YOUR CONSISTENCY OR RELIABILITY:

____

____

____

> IN THE NEXT 6 MONTHS. TARGET DATE: ______________________
>
> A HABIT OR PATTERN OF FAITHFULNESS YOU WANT TO SEE FIRMLY ESTABLISHED:

____

____

____

____

> IN THE NEXT YEAR. TARGET DATE: ______________________
>
> THE KIND OF LEADER YOU HOPE TO BECOME AS FAITHFULNESS SHAPES YOUR LIFE:

____

____

____

____

Anticipating Challenges

> WHAT PRESSURES, DISTRACTIONS, OR ATTITUDES MIGHT HINDER YOUR FAITHFULNESS?

> HOW WILL YOU RESPOND WHEN THOSE CHALLENGES ARISE?

Evidence of Growth

> WHAT SIGNS WOULD SHOW THAT TRUSTWORTHINESS IS INCREASING IN YOUR LEADERSHIP?

> WHAT VISIBLE OUTCOMES WOULD REFLECT GREATER FAITHFULNESS IN YOUR RESPONSIBILITIES?

Reflection and Learning

After some time has passed, return to this page and reflect on what you experienced as you applied this principle.

> WHAT WENT WELL AS YOU PRACTICED FAITHFULNESS?

> WHAT DID YOU LEARN ABOUT YOUR CONSISTENCY OR RELIABILITY?

> WHAT STILL NEEDS IMPROVEMENT OR DEEPER ATTENTION?

> WHAT WILL BE YOUR NEXT STEP FOR CONTINUED GROWTH?

BIBLICAL PORTRAIT

DANIEL

FAITHFULNESS UNDER PRESSURE

DANIEL stands as a powerful example of trustworthiness and faithfulness in leadership.

Taken into exile in Babylon, Daniel found himself serving in a foreign government under rulers who did not share his beliefs. Yet even in this environment, Daniel distinguished himself through integrity, discipline, and unwavering faithfulness.

Scripture tells us that he was found trustworthy, with no corruption or negligence in him (Daniel 6:4). His work was so consistent and reliable that even those who sought to accuse him could find no fault in his conduct.

Daniel's greatest test came when a decree was issued forbidding prayer to anyone except the king. For Daniel, this created a direct conflict between obedience to God and obedience to authority.

Yet Daniel did not change his behavior. He continued to pray openly, just as he had always done. His faithfulness did not depend on convenience or safety. It was rooted in conviction.

As a result, Daniel was thrown into the lions' den. Yet even in that moment, God honored his faithfulness and preserved his life.

Daniel's story reminds us that true trustworthiness is revealed under pressure. It is easy to be consistent when circumstances are favorable, but faithfulness is proven when it becomes costly.

In leadership and business, the same principle applies. Trust is built when leaders remain steady, reliable, and committed to what is right, even when it is difficult.

Faithfulness over time creates a reputation that others can depend on—and a life that honors God.

07

Those who listen to godly counsel walk in safety; those who act alone risk falling into error.

SEEKING COUNSEL

Wise decisions are built on shared wisdom.

Seeking counsel is an act of humility and wisdom. It acknowledges that no one has all the answers—not even the most capable leader. The Bible repeatedly affirms that wisdom grows through community and conversation.

In business and leadership, seeking godly counsel prevents rash decisions and provides clarity when emotions or ambition might cloud judgment. Wise leaders surround themselves with advisors who speak truth, not just agreement. Above all, they seek God's voice as the ultimate Counselor, trusting that He directs every step.

BIBLICAL FOUNDATION

Proverbs 15:22

"WITHOUT COUNSEL PLANS FAIL, BUT WITH MANY ADVISERS THEY SUCCEED."

This proverb reminds us that success is rarely the result of isolated thinking. Even the best ideas benefit from outside perspective. In business, inviting counsel helps uncover blind spots, refine strategy, and strengthen decision-making. Wisdom grows when plans are tested, discussed, and shaped through the insight of others rather than carried alone.

Proverbs 11:14

"WHERE THERE IS NO GUIDANCE, A PEOPLE FALLS, BUT IN AN ABUNDANCE OF COUNSELORS THERE IS SAFETY."

Here, Scripture emphasizes protection as one of the great benefits of counsel. Guidance provides stability, especially during seasons of uncertainty or change. In the business world, trusted advisors and collaborative leadership act as safeguards—helping organizations navigate challenges, avoid costly missteps, and move forward with confidence rather than haste.

James 1:5

"IF ANY OF YOU LACKS WISDOM, LET HIM ASK GOD, WHO GIVES GENEROUSLY TO ALL WITHOUT REPROACH, AND IT WILL BE GIVEN HIM."

While human counsel is invaluable, this verse reminds us that wisdom ultimately begins with God. When decisions feel complex or unclear, leaders are invited to seek divine guidance with humility and trust. In business, this means recognizing the limits of human understanding and anchoring decisions in prayer, discernment, and dependence on God's generosity.

Together, these passages present counsel as both practical and spiritual. Wise leadership welcomes the insight of others, values diverse perspectives, and remains attentive to God's direction. In business, this approach leads to clearer judgment, healthier leadership, and greater stability over time. When counsel is embraced—not resisted—decisions are strengthened, risks are reduced, and success becomes far more sustainable.

THE POWER OF SHARED WISDOM

John Henderson, a Christian entrepreneur, stood on the threshold of a major decision: expanding his growing gourmet coffee chain. The opportunity was exciting—but risky. Remembering the importance of seeking counsel, John gathered a group of trusted advisors before moving forward.

Among them were his long-time mentor, a seasoned strategist, and a financial analyst. Each one brought unique experience and perspective to the table. They discussed market data, funding options, and potential challenges. John's mentor reminded him of Proverbs 15:22: "Without counsel plans fail, but with many advisers they succeed."

As they talked, the strategist warned about market saturation, and the analyst advised a conservative investment approach. Their insights revealed factors John had overlooked. What could have been a reckless leap became a carefully planned step of faith.

Still, John knew that even the best human wisdom wasn't enough. Before making his final decision, he sought divine direction, praying through James 1:5 and asking God for clarity and peace. With both spiritual and practical counsel, he moved forward confidently.

The expansion succeeded beyond expectations. More than profit, it confirmed a timeless truth: success is rarely a solo journey. God blesses those who walk with wise advisors and a humble heart that seeks His guidance above all.

WISDOM TO BUILD ON

Godly counsel brings clarity, safety, and success.

Humility invites wisdom; pride isolates.

Seek advisors who value truth more than approval.

The wisest leader listens—to people and to God.

BLUEPRINT FOR TODAY

Before making any major decision, pause and seek counsel. Gather trusted voices who will speak honestly, not flatteringly. Then, seek God's wisdom above all others.

Ask God to help you see whose wisdom He has placed around you—and to give you discernment to listen, learn, and act according to His will.

BUILD YOUR BLUEPRINT

Honest Self-Assessment

Wise leadership recognizes the need for guidance.

It is easy to believe we must have all the answers or carry every responsibility alone. Yet Scripture teaches that wisdom grows through counsel, and that seeking guidance is not weakness—it is strength.

Take a moment to reflect honestly.

> DO YOU TEND TO MAKE DECISIONS INDEPENDENTLY, OR DO YOU REGULARLY SEEK COUNSEL FROM OTHERS?

____

____

____

____

____

____

> ARE THERE AREAS WHERE PRIDE OR FEAR HAS KEPT YOU FROM ASKING FOR ADVICE?

____

____

____

____

____

> WHERE COULD SEEKING WISE COUNSEL IMPROVE YOUR DECISIONS OR LEADERSHIP?

____

____

____

____

____

Reflection Before God

God often speaks through wise and trusted people.

Seeking counsel requires humility—the willingness to listen, to learn, and sometimes to change direction. Scripture reminds us that in the multitude of counselors there is safety.

Take time to reflect prayerfully.

> What part of this chapter most challenged your approach to decision-making?

____

____

____

____

____

> In what area of your leadership do you sense God inviting you to seek guidance?

____

____

____

____

____

> Write a short prayer.
> Ask God to give you a humble and teachable heart that seeks wisdom from Him and from others.

____

____

____

____

____

____

____

____

Strategic Implementation

Seeking counsel becomes practical when we intentionally invite wisdom into our decisions.

Leaders who seek counsel avoid unnecessary mistakes and make stronger, more balanced decisions.

> ONE AREA WHERE I WILL INTENTIONALLY SEEK COUNSEL:

____

____

____

____

____

> A PERSON I CAN APPROACH FOR WISE ADVICE OR PERSPECTIVE:

____

____

____

____

____

> A STEP I CAN TAKE TO BUILD A HABIT OF SEEKING COUNSEL:

____

____

____

____

____

> ONE DECISION THIS WEEK WHERE I WILL NOT ACT ALONE:

____

____

____

____

____

Growth and Accountability

Wisdom grows when we consistently seek and apply counsel.

> WHO COULD HELP ENCOURAGE YOU TO REMAIN TEACHABLE AND OPEN TO ADVICE?

____

Define Your Growth Milestones

> IN THE NEXT 30 DAYS. TARGET DATE: ______________________
A SMALL BUT MEANINGFUL STEP TOWARD SEEKING COUNSEL:

____

____

____

> IN THE NEXT 90 DAYS. TARGET DATE: ______________________
A VISIBLE CHANGE IN HOW YOU INVOLVE OTHERS IN YOUR DECISIONS:

____

____

____

> IN THE NEXT 6 MONTHS. TARGET DATE: ______________________
A HABIT OR STRUCTURE OF COUNSEL YOU WANT TO ESTABLISH
(MENTORS, ADVISORS, TEAM INPUT):

____

____

____

____

> IN THE NEXT YEAR. TARGET DATE: ______________________
THE KIND OF LEADER YOU HOPE TO BECOME AS YOU GROW IN WISDOM AND HUMILITY:

____

____

____

____

Anticipating Challenges

> What attitudes or fears might keep you from seeking counsel?

____

____

____

____

____

> How will you respond when those challenges arise?

____

____

____

____

____

Evidence of Growth

> What signs would show that you are becoming more teachable and wise in your decisions?

____

____

____

____

____

____

> What visible outcomes would reflect better decision-making through counsel?

____

____

____

____

____

Reflection and Learning

After some time has passed, return to this page and reflect on what you experienced as you applied this principle.

> WHAT WENT WELL AS YOU SOUGHT COUNSEL?

> WHAT DID YOU LEARN FROM OTHERS THAT YOU MIGHT HAVE MISSED ON YOUR OWN?

> WHAT STILL NEEDS IMPROVEMENT OR DEEPER ATTENTION?

> WHAT WILL BE YOUR NEXT STEP FOR CONTINUED GROWTH?

Biblical Portrait

Moses

Wisdom Through Counsel

MOSES was a faithful and capable leader, chosen by God to lead the people of Israel out of Egypt. Yet even strong leaders can become overwhelmed when they try to carry every responsibility alone.

In Exodus 18, Moses spent long days judging disputes among the people. From morning until evening, he handled every case himself. His father-in-law Jethro observed this and recognized that the burden was too great.

Jethro offered wise counsel. He told Moses that what he was doing was not sustainable—that both he and the people would become exhausted. He advised Moses to delegate responsibility by appointing capable leaders over groups of people, allowing them to handle smaller matters while Moses focused on what was most important. This was not a correction of Moses' character, but a refinement of his leadership.

Moses had a choice: continue leading alone, or humbly receive counsel. He listened.

Moses implemented Jethro's advice, creating structure, delegation, and shared responsibility among the people. As a result, the burden was lifted, and the leadership of Israel became more effective and sustainable.

Moses' example reminds us that even God-appointed leaders need wise counsel. Seeking advice does not diminish leadership—it strengthens it. Leaders who listen well gain clarity, avoid burnout, and make better decisions.

Wisdom often comes not from having all the answers, but from being willing to receive them.

08

To deal honestly, treat people equally, and defend the vulnerable is to mirror His righteousness in a world that often values gain over goodness.

JUSTICE AND FAIRNESS

Justice and fairness reflect the heart of God.

Justice and fairness are not optional virtues—they are central to God's character. Scripture shows that He delights in truth, defends the oppressed, and demands honesty in all dealings. As His representatives, believers are called to model this same integrity.

In business, justice and fairness shape how we measure success. They require honesty in transactions, equity in leadership, and compassion toward those under our care. When fairness governs our work, trust is built, and God's favor rests upon what we do.

BIBLICAL FOUNDATION

Proverbs 11:1

"THE LORD DETESTS DISHONEST SCALES, BUT ACCURATE WEIGHTS FIND FAVOR WITH HIM."

This proverb speaks plainly about God's concern for fairness and truth. Integrity in business is not a minor detail—it matters deeply to Him. Honest practices, transparent transactions, and accuracy in dealings reflect a heart committed to justice. In the marketplace, fairness builds trust, strengthens relationships, and establishes credibility that cannot be manufactured through marketing or success alone.

Colossians 4:1

"MASTERS, PROVIDE YOUR SLAVES WITH WHAT IS RIGHT AND FAIR, BECAUSE YOU KNOW THAT YOU ALSO HAVE A MASTER IN HEAVEN."

This verse reminds those in positions of authority that leadership comes with responsibility. Power is never meant to be exercised without accountability. In business, this means treating employees, partners, and collaborators with dignity, fairness, and respect. Leaders are called to remember that they, too, answer to God—and that awareness should shape how decisions are made and people are treated.

James 2:1–4

"BELIEVERS IN OUR GLORIOUS LORD JESUS CHRIST MUST NOT SHOW FAVORITISM... HAVE YOU NOT DISCRIMINATED AMONG YOURSELVES AND BECOME JUDGES WITH EVIL THOUGHTS?"

James confronts the tendency to judge others based on appearance, status, or perceived value. Favoritism distorts justice and undermines community. In a business context, this passage challenges leaders to act impartially—making decisions based on truth, character, and merit rather than wealth, influence, or convenience. Fairness requires seeing people not as assets or liabilities, but as individuals worthy of equal respect.

Together, these passages form a strong biblical framework for justice and fairness in the workplace. They call for honesty in transactions, righteousness in leadership, and impartiality in relationships. When businesses embrace these values, they create environments marked by trust, respect, and integrity. Justice rooted in Scripture does more than prevent harm—it reflects the compassionate and righteous character of God and lays the foundation for lasting, honorable success.

BUILDING A BUSINESS OF INTEGRITY

In the vibrant city of Lagos, Nigeria, two Christian business partners, Chinedu and Ada, founded Integrity Ventures with a clear mission: to build a company rooted in biblical justice and fairness. From day one, they pledged that their business would honor God through honesty, equality, and respect for all.

They began by putting Proverbs 11:1 into action. Investing in high-quality weighing equipment, they ensured that every product was measured accurately and transparently. Their commitment to honest trade built trust with both customers and suppliers, earning their company a sterling reputation in a competitive market.

As Integrity Ventures grew, Chinedu and Ada remembered Colossians 4:1. They made fair wages and safe working conditions a non-negotiable standard. Their employees came from diverse backgrounds, and each one was treated with dignity and given opportunities for growth. "We may be the owners," Ada often said, "but we serve the same Master in heaven."

In meetings, James 2:1–4 served as a guiding principle. Chinedu would remind the team: "No client is more important than another. No voice in this room is less valuable." Their rejection of favoritism fostered a culture of respect and inclusion that transformed their workplace into a community.

Over time, Integrity Ventures became known not only for quality products but for quality character. Their story proved that justice and fairness are not just ideals—they are strategies for godly success. Businesses built on righteousness stand firm because they reflect the God who never changes.

WISDOM TO BUILD ON

Justice honors God and blesses people.

Fairness in leadership builds trust and loyalty.

Honesty in small things protects credibility in big things.

Equality and respect turn workplaces into communities.

BLUEPRINT FOR TODAY

Choose integrity in every decision, even when it costs you. Treat everyone—employees, clients, and competitors—with fairness and dignity. Let your leadership reflect the justice of your Master in heaven.

Ask God to help you see where favoritism or unfairness may have crept in—and to make your work a reflection of His perfect righteousness.

BUILD YOUR BLUEPRINT

Honest Self-Assessment

Justice and fairness are essential to godly leadership.

Leaders are entrusted with authority that affects others, and Scripture calls them to exercise that authority with integrity, impartiality, and compassion. Justice ensures what is right; fairness ensures people are treated rightly.

Take a moment to reflect honestly.

> DO YOU TEND TO MAKE DECISIONS BASED ON WHAT IS RIGHT, OR ON WHAT IS EASIEST OR MOST BENEFICIAL?

____

____

____

____

____

____

> ARE THERE SITUATIONS WHERE YOU HAVE SHOWN FAVORITISM OR AVOIDED DIFFICULT BUT FAIR DECISIONS?

____

____

____

____

____

> WHERE COULD GREATER FAIRNESS STRENGTHEN TRUST IN YOUR LEADERSHIP OR ORGANIZATION?

____

____

____

____

____

Reflection Before God

God is just and calls His people to reflect His character in how they lead and treat others.

Justice is not only about rules—it is about honoring what is right in God's sight. Fairness requires humility, courage, and a willingness to act with integrity, even when it is uncomfortable.

> WHAT PART OF THIS CHAPTER MOST CHALLENGED YOUR UNDERSTANDING OF JUSTICE OR FAIRNESS?

____

____

____

____

____

> IN WHAT AREA DO YOU FEEL GOD CALLING YOU TO ACT MORE JUSTLY OR FAIRLY?

____

____

____

____

____

> WRITE A SHORT PRAYER.
> ASK GOD TO GUIDE YOUR DECISIONS SO THAT THEY REFLECT TRUTH, FAIRNESS, AND COMPASSION.

____

____

____

____

____

____

____

____

Strategic Implementation

Justice and fairness become visible through consistent decisions. Leaders who act justly create environments of trust, respect, and accountability.

> ONE AREA WHERE I NEED TO ACT MORE JUSTLY OR FAIRLY:

> A SITUATION WHERE I NEED TO MAKE A FAIR DECISION, EVEN IF IT IS DIFFICULT:

> A STEP I CAN TAKE TO ENSURE IMPARTIALITY IN MY LEADERSHIP:

> A HABIT I CAN DEVELOP TO CONSISTENTLY ACT WITH FAIRNESS:

Growth and Accountability

Justice grows through consistent and courageous decisions over time.

> WHO COULD HELP HOLD YOU ACCOUNTABLE AS YOU GROW IN THIS AREA?

____

Define Your Growth Milestones

> IN THE NEXT 30 DAYS. TARGET DATE: ______________________

A SMALL BUT MEANINGFUL STEP TOWARD GREATER FAIRNESS:

____

____

____

> IN THE NEXT 90 DAYS. TARGET DATE: ______________________

A VISIBLE IMPROVEMENT IN HOW YOU MAKE JUST DECISIONS:

____

____

____

> IN THE NEXT 6 MONTHS. TARGET DATE: ______________________

A SYSTEM OR CULTURE OF FAIRNESS YOU WANT TO ESTABLISH:

____

____

____

____

> IN THE NEXT YEAR. TARGET DATE: ______________________

THE KIND OF LEADER YOU HOPE TO BECOME AS JUSTICE SHAPES YOUR LEADERSHIP:

____

____

____

____

Anticipating Challenges

> WHAT PRESSURES OR FEARS MIGHT MAKE IT DIFFICULT TO ACT JUSTLY?

> HOW WILL YOU RESPOND WHEN THOSE CHALLENGES ARISE?

Evidence of Growth

> WHAT SIGNS WOULD SHOW THAT JUSTICE AND FAIRNESS ARE INCREASING IN YOUR LEADERSHIP?

> WHAT VISIBLE OUTCOMES WOULD REFLECT A CULTURE OF FAIRNESS IN YOUR ORGANIZATION?

Reflection and Learning

After some time has passed, return to this page and reflect on what you experienced as you applied this principle.

> WHAT WENT WELL AS YOU PRACTICED JUSTICE AND FAIRNESS?

> WHAT DID YOU LEARN ABOUT YOUR DECISIONS OR LEADERSHIP?

> WHAT STILL NEEDS IMPROVEMENT OR DEEPER ATTENTION?

> WHAT WILL BE YOUR NEXT STEP FOR CONTINUED GROWTH?

BIBLICAL PORTRAIT

BOAZ

JUSTICE WITH COMPASSION

BOAZ stands as a powerful example of justice and fairness lived out with integrity and compassion.

In the book of Ruth, Boaz is introduced as a man of standing and influence, yet his leadership is marked not by power alone, but by righteousness. When Ruth, a foreign widow, came to glean in his fields, Boaz ensured she was treated with dignity and respect. He followed the law that allowed the poor to gather leftover grain, but he went beyond what was required by showing kindness and protection.

Boaz's commitment to justice becomes even clearer when he takes responsibility as a kinsman-redeemer. According to the law, a relative had the right to redeem Ruth and Naomi's land. Boaz did not act impulsively or unfairly. Instead, he brought the matter before the elders at the city gate, ensuring that everything was handled openly and according to what was right.

Even when another man had the first right to redeem, Boaz honored the process. Only after the other man declined did Boaz step forward to fulfill the responsibility himself.

Boaz shows us that true justice is not only about doing what is legally correct, but about doing what is right in both action and heart.

In leadership and business, fairness requires integrity, transparency, and a willingness to act with both truth and compassion. Boaz reminds us that leaders who uphold justice while caring for others create trust, honor, and lasting impact.

09

When we lower ourselves before God and others, He lifts us up to serve with wisdom, grace, and influence.

HUMILITY

True greatness begins with humility.

Humility is not weakness—it is strength submitted to God. It is the quiet confidence that acknowledges, "Without Him, I can do nothing." In leadership, humility brings perspective. It allows us to learn, to listen, and to lead others with compassion rather than control.

In business, humility transforms culture. It breaks down pride, invites collaboration, and builds trust. The humble leader doesn't seek to prove their worth; they create space for others to shine. And in doing so, they reflect the very nature of Christ, who "made Himself nothing, taking the very nature of a servant." (Philippians 2:7)

BIBLICAL FOUNDATION

Philippians 2:3–4

"DO NOTHING OUT OF SELFISH AMBITION OR VAIN CONCEIT. RATHER, IN HUMILITY VALUE OTHERS ABOVE YOURSELVES, NOT LOOKING TO YOUR OWN INTERESTS BUT EACH OF YOU TO THE INTERESTS OF THE OTHERS."

This passage calls us to examine the motives behind our actions. Humility is not about diminishing ourselves, but about making room for others. In a work environment, this posture transforms how teams function. When people look beyond personal gain and consider the needs of those around them, collaboration deepens, trust grows, and a culture of mutual support begins to take shape.

Proverbs 22:4

"HUMILITY IS THE FEAR OF THE LORD; ITS WAGES ARE RICHES AND HONOR AND LIFE."

Proverbs connects humility with reverence for God, showing that it is not weakness but wisdom. Leaders who walk humbly recognize that their abilities, opportunities, and success ultimately come from Him. In business, this kind of humility fosters teachability, steadiness, and respect. Over time, it builds credibility and lays a foundation for success that is both meaningful and lasting.

James 4:10

"HUMBLE YOURSELVES BEFORE THE LORD, AND HE WILL LIFT YOU UP."

James reminds us that promotion and recognition are not self-made achievements. True elevation comes from God. In the workplace, this truth encourages leaders to resist self-promotion and instead focus on faithfulness, service, and integrity. When humility guides leadership, growth and advancement follow in God's timing and in His way.

Together, these Scriptures present humility as an essential quality for healthy leadership and effective teamwork. By valuing others, acknowledging limitations, and serving with sincerity, individuals help cultivate workplaces marked by respect, unity, and purpose. Biblical humility not only strengthens relationships—it creates space for personal growth, shared success, and the kind of advancement that aligns with God's promises.

LEADING WITH LISTENING

In the fast-moving world of technology, few transformations are as striking as that of Microsoft under the leadership of Satya Nadella. When he became CEO in 2014, the company was struggling—stuck in prideful competition and internal silos. Nadella, a Christian man shaped by the principle of humility, chose a different path.

Rather than asserting authority, he began by listening. He met with teams across every department, asking questions and valuing their ideas. He admitted where he didn't have all the answers—a posture of leadership that echoed Proverbs 22:4: "Humility is the fear of the Lord; its wages are riches and honor and life."

By putting people first, Nadella revived the heart of the organization. His leadership reflected Philippians 2:3–4, fostering collaboration instead of competition. Teams began to innovate fearlessly, empowered by trust and mutual respect.

When reporters asked about his success, Nadella often pointed back to a simple truth: "Empathy makes you a better innovator." In essence, he lived James 4:10: "Humble yourselves before the Lord, and He will lift you up." Microsoft not only recovered—it flourished, becoming one of the most valuable and forward-thinking companies in the world.

Nadella's story illustrates a powerful truth: humility doesn't hold us back—it propels us forward under God's hand. Those who serve others with sincerity often find themselves elevated in ways they never pursued.

WISDOM TO BUILD ON

Humility invites God's wisdom and favor.

Listening is the language of a humble heart.

Great leaders lift others higher.

The path to honor begins with surrender.

BLUEPRINT FOR TODAY

Lead today with open hands and an open heart. Be willing to learn, to listen, and to give credit where it's due. Let humility define your leadership, knowing that every promotion worth having comes from God alone.

Ask God to help you see where pride may be hiding in your heart—and to replace it with the joy and freedom that come from humility before Him.

BUILD YOUR BLUEPRINT

Honest Self-Assessment

Humility is the foundation of godly leadership.

In leadership and business, it is easy to seek recognition, control, or personal advancement. Yet Scripture teaches that true leadership is marked by humility—a willingness to submit to God and to serve others.

Take a moment to reflect honestly.

> DO YOU TEND TO SEEK RECOGNITION FOR YOUR WORK, OR ARE YOU CONTENT TO SERVE WITHOUT BEING NOTICED?

____

____

____

____

____

____

> IN WHAT AREAS MIGHT PRIDE INFLUENCE YOUR DECISIONS, ATTITUDES, OR RELATIONSHIPS?

____

____

____

____

____

> WHERE COULD GREATER HUMILITY STRENGTHEN YOUR LEADERSHIP AND RELATIONSHIPS?

____

____

____

____

____

Reflection Before God

Humility begins with recognizing our dependence on God.

Scripture reminds us that God resists the proud but gives grace to the humble. A humble leader understands that every ability, opportunity, and success comes from Him.

Take time to reflect prayerfully.

> WHAT PART OF THIS CHAPTER MOST CHALLENGED YOUR UNDERSTANDING OF HUMILITY?

____

____

____

____

____

> IN WHAT AREA DO YOU SENSE GOD CALLING YOU TO SURRENDER PRIDE AND GROW IN HUMILITY?

____

____

____

____

____

> WRITE A SHORT PRAYER.
> ASK GOD TO SHAPE YOUR HEART SO THAT HUMILITY BECOMES A DEFINING CHARACTERISTIC OF YOUR LEADERSHIP.

____

____

____

____

____

____

____

____

Strategic Implementation

Humility becomes visible through our attitudes and actions.

Leaders who walk in humility listen well, value others, and recognize that leadership is a responsibility, not a privilege.

> ONE AREA WHERE I NEED TO PRACTICE HUMILITY IMMEDIATELY:

> A SITUATION WHERE I NEED TO LISTEN MORE AND SPEAK LESS:

> A STEP I CAN TAKE TO VALUE AND HONOR OTHERS IN MY LEADERSHIP:

> A HABIT I CAN BEGIN THIS WEEK THAT REFLECTS A HUMBLE MINDSET:

Growth and Accountability

Humility grows through intentional surrender and consistent practice.

> WHO COULD HELP HOLD YOU ACCOUNTABLE AS YOU GROW IN THIS AREA?

____

Define Your Growth Milestones

> IN THE NEXT 30 DAYS. TARGET DATE: ______________________
> A SMALL BUT MEANINGFUL STEP TOWARD GREATER HUMILITY:

____

____

____

> IN THE NEXT 90 DAYS. TARGET DATE: ______________________
> A VISIBLE CHANGE IN YOUR ATTITUDE OR INTERACTIONS WITH OTHERS:

____

____

____

> IN THE NEXT 6 MONTHS. TARGET DATE: ______________________
> A HABIT OR LEADERSHIP CULTURE YOU WANT TO SEE DEVELOPING:

____

____

____

____

> IN THE NEXT YEAR. TARGET DATE: ______________________
> THE KIND OF LEADER YOU HOPE TO BECOME AS HUMILITY SHAPES YOUR LIFE:

____

____

____

____

Anticipating Challenges

> WHAT SITUATIONS OR ATTITUDES MIGHT CAUSE PRIDE TO RISE IN YOUR LEADERSHIP?

> HOW WILL YOU RESPOND WHEN THOSE CHALLENGES ARISE?

Evidence of Growth

> WHAT SIGNS WOULD SHOW THAT HUMILITY IS INCREASING IN YOUR LEADERSHIP?

> WHAT VISIBLE CHANGES WOULD REFLECT A MORE HUMBLE LEADERSHIP CULTURE?

Reflection and Learning

After some time has passed, return to this page and reflect on what you experienced as you applied this principle.

> WHAT WENT WELL AS YOU PRACTICED HUMILITY?

____

____

____

____

____

> WHAT DID YOU LEARN ABOUT YOUR HEART OR LEADERSHIP?

____

____

____

____

____

> WHAT STILL NEEDS IMPROVEMENT OR DEEPER ATTENTION?

____

____

____

____

____

> WHAT WILL BE YOUR NEXT STEP FOR CONTINUED GROWTH?

____

____

____

____

____

____

Biblical Portrait

David

Humility Before God and Others

DAVID'S life offers a powerful example of humility in leadership.

Even after being anointed as king, David did not seize power. Instead, he continued serving faithfully and waited for God's timing. When King Saul pursued him unjustly, David had multiple opportunities to take Saul's life. Yet he refused, recognizing Saul as the Lord's anointed.

David chose humility over ambition.

He trusted God to establish him in His time, rather than forcing his own path forward.

David's humility is also seen in his relationship with God. When he sinned, he did not justify himself or shift blame. Instead, he responded with repentance and a broken heart before God (Psalm 51).

He understood that leadership did not make him greater—it made him more dependent on God's grace.

David's life reminds us that humility is not weakness. It is strength under control, guided by trust in God.

In leadership and business, humility allows us to lead with patience, to honor others, and to recognize that success ultimately comes from God. Leaders who walk in humility build trust, receive grace, and create environments where others can grow.

True greatness is not found in exalting ourselves, but in submitting ourselves to God.

10

When we align our plans with His will, our work becomes more than success—it becomes significance.

VISION AND PURPOSE

God's vision gives direction; His purpose gives meaning.

Vision and purpose begin with seeing life—and work—through God's eyes. A biblical vision isn't about personal ambition; it's about discerning what God wants to accomplish through us. Purpose flows from that vision. It calls us to serve, to build, and to influence for His glory, not our gain.

In business, a God-centered vision transforms profit into purpose. It guides decisions, motivates teams, and creates long-term impact that outlasts trends or circumstances. A company guided by divine vision becomes a vessel of provision, service, and light in its community.

BIBLICAL FOUNDATION

Colossians 3:23–24

"WHATEVER YOU DO, WORK AT IT WITH ALL YOUR HEART, AS WORKING FOR THE LORD, NOT FOR HUMAN MASTERS, SINCE YOU KNOW THAT YOU WILL RECEIVE AN INHERITANCE FROM THE LORD AS A REWARD. IT IS THE LORD CHRIST YOU ARE SERVING."

These verses remind us that work is never merely transactional. When our efforts are offered with sincerity and excellence, they become an expression of service to God. In business, this perspective shapes both attitude and conduct. It encourages integrity, diligence, and care—not because someone is watching, but because our work reflects who we serve. Purpose-filled work elevates everyday responsibilities into meaningful contributions.

Proverbs 29:18

> "WHERE THERE IS NO VISION, THE PEOPLE PERISH: BUT HE THAT KEEPETH THE LAW, HAPPY IS HE."

This proverb highlights how essential vision is for direction and vitality. Vision provides clarity—it helps people understand why they are doing what they do and where they are going. In a business context, a clear vision guides decisions, aligns efforts, and keeps an organization focused when challenges arise. Without it, even well-intentioned work can drift, losing momentum and purpose over time.

Jeremiah 29:11

> "FOR I KNOW THE PLANS I HAVE FOR YOU," DECLARES THE LORD, "PLANS FOR WELFARE AND NOT FOR EVIL, TO GIVE YOU A FUTURE AND A HOPE."

Jeremiah's words offer reassurance that God's purposes extend into every area of life, including our work and leadership. This promise invites trust—especially when outcomes are uncertain. In business, it encourages leaders to pursue ventures that align with God's heart for good, welfare, and hope. Rather than chasing success at any cost, it calls for building with long-term impact and concern for others.

Together, these Scriptures form a strong foundation for understanding vision and purpose in business. A God-centered vision brings direction, integrity shapes the way work is done, and trust in God's plans sustains leaders through uncertainty. When organizations anchor their practices in these truths, they are better equipped to pursue success that is sustainable, meaningful, and beneficial to the communities they serve. Biblical vision does more than define goals—it gives work lasting significance and aligns leadership with God's greater purpose.

A VISION ROOTED IN FAITH

In 1914, James Cash Penney founded the J.C. Penney Company with a vision grounded firmly in his Christian faith. He believed that business could—and should—be a ministry, guided by the Golden Rule: "Do unto others as you would have them do unto you." This conviction shaped everything his company stood for—honesty, service, and respect for both employees and customers.

When the Great Depression devastated countless businesses, Penney's vision held firm. Though his company faced severe trials, he continued to prioritize ethical practices, fair wages, and genuine care for others. He trusted Jeremiah 29:11, believing that God's plan for his company extended beyond immediate profit to long-term blessing.

Penney also embodied Colossians 3:23–24, approaching his work as service to the Lord rather than mere pursuit of success. His humility and faith sustained him through hardship, and his company not only survived—it thrived. Communities across America benefited from his generosity and steadfast leadership.

His legacy endures today, a testament that when vision and purpose are aligned with Scripture, business becomes more than a livelihood—it becomes a mission.

WISDOM TO BUILD ON

Success aligned with God's plan blesses both people and generations.

Faithful leaders pursue impact, not applause.

Godly vision brings direction and hope.

Purpose transforms ordinary work into ministry.

BLUEPRINT FOR TODAY

Seek God's vision before setting your goals. Ask Him to clarify His purpose for your work, your business, and your influence. Then, pursue that purpose with diligence and faith.

Ask God to help you see beyond the temporary and to align every plan with His eternal vision, trusting that His way always leads to lasting fruit.

BUILD YOUR BLUEPRINT

Honest Self-Assessment

Vision gives direction, and purpose gives meaning to leadership.

Without a clear vision, leaders may stay busy but lack direction. Without purpose, even success can feel empty. Scripture shows that God gives vision not just for achievement, but for fulfillment of His purposes.

Take a moment to reflect honestly.

> Do you have a clear sense of vision and purpose in your leadership or work?

> Are you currently moving with intention, or reacting to circumstances?

> Where might a lack of clarity be limiting your effectiveness or direction?

Reflection Before God

God is the source of true vision.

Throughout Scripture, vision begins when leaders align their hearts with God's purposes. Vision is not simply about personal ambition—it is about participating in what God is doing.

Take time to reflect prayerfully.

> What part of this chapter most challenged your understanding of vision or purpose?

> Where do you sense God directing your focus or calling your attention?

> Write a short prayer.
> Ask God to clarify your vision and align your purpose with His will.

Strategic Implementation

Vision becomes meaningful when it is translated into action.

Leaders with clear purpose move intentionally, communicate direction, and inspire others to move forward together.

> ONE AREA WHERE I NEED GREATER CLARITY OF VISION:

> A STEP I CAN TAKE TO BETTER DEFINE OR COMMUNICATE MY PURPOSE:

> ONE ACTION I CAN TAKE TO MOVE FORWARD WITH CLARITY THIS WEEK:

> A HABIT I CAN BEGIN THAT HELPS ME STAY FOCUSED ON WHAT MATTERS MOST:

Growth and Accountability

Vision grows stronger as it is pursued consistently over time.

> WHO COULD HELP HOLD YOU ACCOUNTABLE AS YOU PURSUE THIS VISION?

____

Define Your Growth Milestones

> IN THE NEXT 30 DAYS. TARGET DATE: ______________________
> A SMALL BUT MEANINGFUL STEP TOWARD GREATER CLARITY AND DIRECTION:

____

____

____

> IN THE NEXT 90 DAYS. TARGET DATE: ______________________
> A VISIBLE STEP FORWARD IN PURSUING YOUR PURPOSE:

____

____

____

____

> IN THE NEXT 6 MONTHS. TARGET DATE: ______________________
> A STRUCTURE OR PLAN YOU WANT TO SEE DEVELOPING:

____

____

____

____

> IN THE NEXT YEAR. TARGET DATE: ______________________
> WHERE YOU HOPE TO BE AS YOU WALK IN VISION AND PURPOSE:

____

____

____

____

Anticipating Challenges

> What distractions or obstacles might pull you away from your vision?

> How will you stay focused when those challenges arise?

Evidence of Growth

> What signs would show that you are walking with greater clarity and purpose?

> What visible outcomes would reflect progress toward your vision?

Reflection and Learning

After some time has passed, return to this page and reflect on what you experienced as you pursued this principle.

> WHAT WENT WELL AS YOU MOVED FORWARD WITH VISION?

> WHAT DID YOU LEARN ABOUT YOUR DIRECTION OR PRIORITIES?

> WHAT STILL NEEDS CLARITY OR ADJUSTMENT?

> WHAT WILL BE YOUR NEXT STEP FOR CONTINUED PROGRESS?

Biblical Portrait

Nehemiah

Vision That Rebuilds

NEHEMIAH provides a powerful example of vision guided by purpose. While serving as cupbearer to the king, Nehemiah heard that Jerusalem's walls were broken down and its gates burned. The news deeply affected him. Instead of ignoring the problem, he allowed it to shape his heart and direction.

Vision often begins with burden. Nehemiah prayed, fasted, and sought God before taking action. When the time came, he approached the king with clarity and courage, asking for permission and resources to rebuild the city.

But Nehemiah's vision did not stop at desire—it moved into planning. He assessed the situation carefully, organized the people, and assigned clear responsibilities. Each group worked on a specific portion of the wall, turning vision into coordinated action.

Despite opposition, criticism, and threats, Nehemiah remained focused. He refused distractions and stayed committed to the work, declaring, "I am doing a great work, so that I cannot come down" (Nehemiah 6:3).

Nehemiah's leadership shows that true vision is not only about seeing what could be, but about faithfully working to make it a reality.

In leadership and business, vision gives direction, but purpose gives endurance. Leaders who align their vision with God's purpose, plan carefully, and remain focused can build something that lasts. Vision, when rooted in God's calling, becomes a force that restores, rebuilds, and inspires others to move forward together.

11

Depending on God means trusting His wisdom above our own, believing that His guidance, provision, and timing are perfect in every season.

DEPENDENCE ON GOD

True success begins with surrender.

Dependence on God is not passivity—it's partnership. It means working diligently while trusting completely, making decisions prayerfully, and remembering that every result ultimately belongs to Him.

In business, dependence on God guards us from pride and fear alike. It keeps leaders grounded in humility when things go well and steadfast in faith when challenges arise. When we rely on His wisdom and provision, our work becomes an act of worship, and our peace no longer depends on performance but on His presence.

BIBLICAL FOUNDATION

Proverbs 3:5–6

"TRUST IN THE LORD WITH ALL YOUR HEART AND LEAN NOT ON YOUR OWN UNDERSTANDING; IN ALL YOUR WAYS SUBMIT TO HIM, AND HE WILL MAKE YOUR PATHS STRAIGHT."

This passage invites us into a posture of dependence and humility. Rather than relying solely on our own insight or experience, we are called to place our confidence in God's wisdom and direction. In business, this means acknowledging that not every answer comes from strategy alone. When leaders submit their plans, decisions, and ambitions to God, they open the door for Him to guide their steps with clarity and purpose—even when the path forward is uncertain.

Philippians 4:19

"AND MY GOD WILL MEET ALL YOUR NEEDS ACCORDING TO THE RICHES OF HIS GLORY IN CHRIST JESUS."

Here we are reminded that provision ultimately comes from God. This promise does not remove responsibility or effort, but it anchors our work in trust rather than anxiety. In a business context, it reassures leaders that resources, opportunities, and support are not limited to human capacity alone. Trusting God's provision frees us to lead with generosity, integrity, and confidence instead of fear-driven decisions.

James 1:5

"IF ANY OF YOU LACKS WISDOM, YOU SHOULD ASK GOD, WHO GIVES GENEROUSLY TO ALL WITHOUT FINDING FAULT, AND IT WILL BE GIVEN TO YOU."

James offers a simple yet powerful encouragement: wisdom is available to those who seek it. When challenges arise or decisions feel overwhelming, leaders are not left to figure everything out on their own. God invites us to ask—and promises to give generously. In business, this dependence on divine wisdom shapes discernment, patience, and sound judgment, especially in moments where outcomes are unclear.

Together, these Scriptures present a clear picture of what it means to depend on God in business. Trust replaces self-reliance, prayer becomes part of decision-making, and confidence is rooted in God's provision rather than circumstances. This kind of spiritual dependence brings peace in uncertainty and steadiness in leadership. When business is guided by faith, it becomes aligned with a higher purpose—one marked by wisdom, integrity, and sustainable growth grounded in trust in God.

A LEADER WHO LOOKED UP BEFORE LOOKING AHEAD

In the early 2000s, Starbucks was expanding rapidly, but the fast growth came at a cost. Quality declined, employees lost motivation, and the company's original values began to fade. When Howard Schultz returned as CEO in 2008, he faced an overwhelming challenge: rebuild not just a business, but a culture.

Instead of relying solely on strategy, Schultz sought to lead with conviction and moral clarity. He turned to principles of integrity, stewardship, and care for people—values that align with Proverbs 3:5–6, trusting in something higher than profit to guide the company's renewal.

He reintroduced ethical sourcing, sustainability initiatives, and a renewed focus on community. Like James 1:5 teaches, Schultz pursued wisdom—not merely from analysts or advisors, but from a deeper conviction about doing what was right. Through this values-centered approach, Starbucks recovered, regaining both credibility and customer trust.

While Schultz may not have framed his decisions in explicitly theological terms, his story illustrates a biblical truth: lasting success flows from a heart that seeks guidance beyond itself. Depending on timeless values—and ultimately, on God's direction—builds stability that outlasts circumstance.

WISDOM TO BUILD ON

True leadership begins with surrender, not control.

God provides every resource needed for His purpose.

Wisdom comes to those who ask in faith.

Dependence on God produces peace in uncertainty.

BLUEPRINT FOR TODAY

Bring every decision before God. Submit your plans, goals, and concerns to Him first, trusting that His direction will lead to the right outcome. Work hard, but rest in His faithfulness.

Ask God to help you see where self-reliance has replaced dependence, and to remind you that His wisdom, not your understanding, makes your path straight.

BUILD YOUR BLUEPRINT

Honest Self-Assessment

Dependence on God is the foundation of wise leadership.

It is easy to rely on experience, strategy, or resources. But Scripture consistently shows that true strength comes from trusting God above all else.

Take a moment to reflect honestly.

> WHEN FACING CHALLENGES, WHAT DO YOU TEND TO RELY ON FIRST—YOUR OWN ABILITY OR GOD?

____

____

____

____

____

____

> IN WHAT AREAS OF YOUR LEADERSHIP OR WORK DO YOU STRUGGLE TO FULLY TRUST GOD?

____

____

____

____

____

____

> WHERE MIGHT SELF-RELIANCE BE LIMITING WHAT GOD WANTS TO DO THROUGH YOU?

____

____

____

____

____

Reflection Before God

God invites His people to depend on Him fully.

Dependence is not weakness—it is alignment. It acknowledges that God sees what we cannot, knows what we do not, and is able beyond our limitations.

Take time to reflect prayerfully.

> What part of this chapter most challenged your view of dependence on God?

> Where is God calling you to trust Him more deeply?

> Write a short prayer.
> Ask God to help you rely on Him in every area of your life and leadership.

Strategic Implementation

Dependence on God is expressed through intentional choices.

Leaders who depend on God seek Him before acting, trust Him in uncertainty, and follow His direction even when it is difficult.

> One situation where I need to rely on God instead of myself:

____

____

____

____

____

> A step I can take to seek God's guidance before making decisions:

____

____

____

____

____

> One action I can take this week that reflects trust in God:

____

____

____

____

____

> A habit I can begin to strengthen daily dependence on God:

____

____

____

____

____

Growth and Accountability

Dependence on God grows through consistent practice.

> WHO COULD ENCOURAGE YOU TO SEEK GOD MORE INTENTIONALLY?

____

Define Your Growth Milestones

> IN THE NEXT 30 DAYS. TARGET DATE: ______________________
> A STEP TOWARD GREATER TRUST AND RELIANCE ON GOD:

____

____

____

> IN THE NEXT 90 DAYS. TARGET DATE: ______________________
> A NOTICEABLE SHIFT IN HOW YOU SEEK GOD IN DECISIONS:

____

____

____

____

> IN THE NEXT 6 MONTHS. TARGET DATE: ______________________
> A CONSISTENT PATTERN OF DEPENDENCE IN YOUR LEADERSHIP:

____

____

____

____

> IN THE NEXT YEAR. TARGET DATE: ______________________
> A DEEPER, MORE CONFIDENT TRUST IN GOD'S GUIDANCE:

____

____

____

____

Anticipating Challenges

> WHAT FEARS OR PRESSURES MIGHT TEMPT YOU TO RELY ON YOURSELF INSTEAD OF GOD?

> HOW WILL YOU RESPOND WHEN THOSE PRESSURES ARISE?

Evidence of Growth

> WHAT SIGNS WOULD SHOW THAT YOU ARE GROWING IN DEPENDENCE ON GOD?

> WHAT OUTCOMES MIGHT REFLECT A LIFE LED BY TRUST RATHER THAN CONTROL?

Reflection and Learning

After some time has passed, return to this page and reflect.

> What happened when you chose to depend on God?

> What did you learn about God's faithfulness?

> Where did you still struggle to trust?

> What will be your next step in growing your dependence on Him?

Biblical Portrait

Jehoshaphat

Dependence in the Face of Fear

JEHOSHAPHAT'S story reveals what it means to depend on God in moments of uncertainty. When a vast army came against Judah, Jehoshaphat was afraid—but he did not act in panic. Instead, he set his heart to seek the Lord and called the people to fast and pray (2 Chronicles 20).

He stood before the assembly and openly acknowledged their need: "We do not know what to do, but our eyes are on You." This is the posture of true dependence.

Rather than relying on military strength or strategy, Jehoshaphat trusted God's word. Through a prophet, God declared that the battle would not be theirs, but His.

Jehoshaphat responded with faith. He led the people into battle not with weapons first, but with worship. Singers went ahead of the army, praising God. As they worshiped, God acted.

The enemy forces turned against each other, and Judah experienced victory without having to fight.

Jehoshaphat's leadership shows that dependence on God is not passive—it is active trust. It seeks God first, listens carefully, and obeys with confidence.

In leadership and business, challenges will come that exceed our ability. In those moments, dependence on God becomes the difference between striving and trusting, between fear and faith.

When leaders fix their eyes on God, they discover that He is not only their guide—but their strength, their defender, and their source of victory.

12

When we live with a sense of responsibility before God and others, our actions gain weight, our character gains depth, and our leadership gains trust.

ACCOUNTABILITY

Accountability keeps integrity alive.

Biblical accountability is not about control—it's about growth. It means being answerable to God, to others, and to the values we claim to uphold. It's the humility to admit mistakes, the courage to correct them, and the wisdom to walk in integrity every day.

In business, accountability builds credibility. It creates cultures where honesty is celebrated and trust runs deep. Leaders who welcome accountability invite strength, not weakness. They model transparency that inspires others to follow with confidence.

BIBLICAL FOUNDATION

Luke 16:10

"WHOEVER CAN BE TRUSTED WITH VERY LITTLE CAN ALSO BE TRUSTED WITH MUCH, AND WHOEVER IS DISHONEST WITH VERY LITTLE WILL ALSO BE DISHONEST WITH MUCH."

Jesus reminds us that faithfulness is proven in the small things. Integrity does not suddenly appear when responsibilities increase—it is formed through consistent honesty and diligence in everyday tasks. In business, attention to detail, reliability, and ethical behavior in minor matters lay the foundation for greater trust and leadership opportunities. Reputation is built quietly, one decision at a time.

Proverbs 27:17

"AS IRON SHARPENS IRON, SO ONE PERSON SHARPENS ANOTHER."

This proverb captures the value of healthy accountability within relationships. Growth rarely happens in isolation; it is often shaped through honest interaction, challenge, and encouragement from others. In a business setting, this kind of accountability strengthens teams. When colleagues are willing to speak truth with respect and support one another's development, performance improves and trust deepens. Mutual sharpening leads not to conflict, but to maturity.

Romans 14:12

"SO THEN, EACH OF US WILL GIVE AN ACCOUNT OF OURSELVES TO GOD."

This verse brings accountability into its fullest perspective. Beyond supervisors, policies, or performance reviews, Scripture reminds us that every action ultimately matters before God. In the workplace, this truth calls leaders and employees alike to act responsibly and ethically, even when no one else is watching. It grounds accountability not in fear, but in integrity and reverence for God.

Together, these passages present accountability as both relational and spiritual. Biblical accountability encourages honesty, responsibility, and growth—within teams and within individual hearts. In business, this approach fosters cultures where people challenge one another constructively, act with integrity in all matters, and remain mindful that their work carries moral weight. When accountability is embraced in this way, organizations are strengthened by trust, clarity, and shared responsibility.

THE MERCHANT WHO MADE HONESTY STANDARD

In the late 19th century, American entrepreneur John Wanamaker changed the face of retail. His Philadelphia department store became famous not only for innovation but for integrity. A devoted Christian, Wanamaker believed every business decision was an opportunity to honor God.

Driven by this conviction, he introduced a revolutionary idea: price tags. Before this, prices were negotiated, often unfairly. But Wanamaker insisted that every customer—rich or poor—should pay the same fair price. This simple act of transparency embodied Proverbs 27:17: sharpening his company's ethics and strengthening customer trust.

He also instilled Luke 16:10 in his employees: faithfulness in small duties led to promotion and greater trust. He valued honesty more than skill and often said, "A man's character is his capital." Wanamaker created systems of accountability, encouraging his staff to hold one another to high moral standards.

Even at the peak of his success, Wanamaker remained humble, remembering Romans 14:12: "Each of us will give an account of ourselves to God." His stores became known as places where fairness, honesty, and respect guided every transaction. Through accountability—to God, to his employees, and to his customers—he built a legacy that still influences modern business ethics today.

WISDOM TO BUILD ON

Remember that every choice answers to God first.

Honest relationships refine us like iron sharpening iron.

Accountability strengthens integrity.

Faithfulness in little things builds trust for greater things.

BLUEPRINT FOR TODAY

Welcome accountability. Seek feedback, invite correction, and surround yourself with people who sharpen your faith and your work.

Ask God to help you see where you've resisted accountability, and to give you the humility to walk transparently before Him and others—because real strength grows in the light.

BUILD YOUR BLUEPRINT

Honest Self-Assessment

Accountability keeps integrity alive.

When we live with a sense of responsibility before God and others, our actions gain weight, our character gains depth, and our leadership gains trust.

Take a moment to reflect honestly.

> WHO HAS THE RIGHT TO SPEAK INTO YOUR LIFE AND CHALLENGE YOU WHEN NEEDED?

____

____

____

____

____

____

> ARE THERE AREAS WHERE YOU AVOID ACCOUNTABILITY OR RESIST CORRECTION?

____

____

____

____

____

____

> HOW MIGHT A LACK OF ACCOUNTABILITY BE AFFECTING YOUR GROWTH OR LEADERSHIP?

____

____

____

____

____

Reflection Before God

God designed growth to happen in community.

Accountability is not about control—it is about transformation. It requires humility to receive correction, courage to be honest, and commitment to pursue truth.

Take time to reflect prayerfully.

> WHAT PART OF THIS CHAPTER MOST CHALLENGED YOUR VIEW OF ACCOUNTABILITY?

____

____

____

____

____

> WHERE IS GOD INVITING YOU TO OPEN YOUR LIFE MORE TO OTHERS?

____

____

____

____

____

____

> WRITE A SHORT PRAYER.
> ASK GOD TO GIVE YOU HUMILITY, HONESTY, AND COURAGE TO LIVE ACCOUNTABLE BEFORE HIM AND OTHERS.

____

____

____

____

____

____

____

Strategic Implementation

Accountability becomes real through intentional relationships. Leaders who grow consistently are those who invite others to walk closely with them—people who can encourage, correct, and strengthen them.

> One person I can invite into a deeper level of accountability:

____

____

____

____

____

> A step I can take to create honest and consistent accountability:

____

____

____

____

____

> One area of my life where I need accountability right now:

____

____

____

____

____

> A habit I can begin to practice transparency and openness:

____

____

____

____

____

Growth and Accountability

Accountability strengthens when it is practiced consistently.

> WHO WILL YOU COMMIT TO MEETING WITH REGULARLY FOR ACCOUNTABILITY?

____

Define Your Growth Milestones

> IN THE NEXT 30 DAYS. TARGET DATE: ______________________
A STEP TOWARD BUILDING A MEANINGFUL ACCOUNTABILITY RELATIONSHIP:

____

____

____

> IN THE NEXT 90 DAYS. TARGET DATE: ______________________
A PATTERN OF HONEST CONVERSATIONS AND MUTUAL ENCOURAGEMENT:

____

____

____

____

> IN THE NEXT 6 MONTHS. TARGET DATE: ______________________
A STRONG AND TRUSTED ACCOUNTABILITY STRUCTURE IN YOUR LIFE:

____

____

____

____

> IN THE NEXT YEAR. TARGET DATE: ______________________
A CULTURE OF ACCOUNTABILITY INFLUENCING YOUR LEADERSHIP AND RELATIONSHIPS:

____

____

____

____

Anticipating Challenges

> WHAT FEARS MIGHT KEEP YOU FROM BEING FULLY OPEN WITH OTHERS?

> HOW WILL YOU RESPOND WHEN ACCOUNTABILITY FEELS UNCOMFORTABLE?

Evidence of Growth

> WHAT SIGNS WOULD SHOW THAT ACCOUNTABILITY IS STRENGTHENING YOUR LIFE?

> WHAT VISIBLE CHANGES MIGHT REFLECT GROWTH THROUGH ACCOUNTABILITY?

Reflection and Learning

After some time has passed, return to this page and reflect.

> WHAT HAS BEEN THE IMPACT OF ACCOUNTABILITY IN YOUR LIFE?

> WHAT DID YOU LEARN THROUGH HONEST CONVERSATIONS WITH OTHERS?

> WHERE DID YOU STRUGGLE TO REMAIN OPEN OR CONSISTENT?

> WHAT WILL BE YOUR NEXT STEP IN DEEPENING ACCOUNTABILITY?

BIBLICAL PORTRAIT

PAUL AND BARNABAS

STRENGTH THROUGH PARTNERSHIP

The relationship between Paul and Barnabas illustrates the power of accountability in leadership. From the beginning, Barnabas played a key role in Paul's life. When others were hesitant to accept Paul, Barnabas stood beside him, encouraged him, and helped establish trust within the early church (Acts 9:27).

Their partnership continued as they were sent out together on mission. They traveled, taught, and faced opposition side by side. Their relationship was not only about shared work—it was about mutual strengthening. They challenged one another, supported one another, and remained committed to the mission God had given them. Even in disagreement, accountability remained.

At one point, Paul and Barnabas had a sharp disagreement over John Mark (Acts 15:36–40). Rather than destroying their calling, the disagreement led to multiplication. They went separate ways, continuing the work in different directions.

Later, Paul would again speak positively of Mark, showing growth, maturity, and restored perspective. This reminds us that accountability is not about perfect agreement—it is about faithful growth.

In leadership and business, accountability creates strength. It provides perspective we cannot see on our own. It guards against pride, corrects direction, and strengthens character.

Leaders who walk alone are vulnerable. Leaders who walk with others grow stronger. Accountability, when embraced with humility and grace, becomes one of the most powerful forces for lasting impact.

APPENDIX

A Model for Grace-Filled Communication

WHY COMMUNICATION MATTERS

After exploring twelve biblical principles that shape how we work and lead, one area remains that puts all of them to the test — **how we communicate.**

Leadership, stewardship, integrity, humility — each one is revealed most clearly not in policies or strategies, but in words.

Communication is where the heart of a leader is most visible. Words can **build up or tear down, heal or divide, inspire or discourage.** The difference lies not in eloquence but in intention — in the spirit behind what is said. Scripture reminds us that "out of the abundance of the heart the mouth speaks" (Matthew 12:34), meaning our communication is a reflection of our inner life and our relationship with God.

When our words are guided by love and seasoned with grace, they carry the power to restore trust, strengthen teams, and reflect Christ in our daily interactions. But when they are careless, defensive, or self-centered, they can quickly undo the very principles we aim to live by.

That's why **communication grounded in love and grace is not optional; it's essential.** It is the living expression of the values that define godly leadership.

Over the years, I developed a simple model that helped me keep my communication aligned with Scripture. I call it a *model* because I did not always live it out perfectly — but it consistently brought me back to center. Two key passages became my anchors: **1 Corinthians 13:4–8**, which defines the *heart* of love, and **Ephesians 4:29**, which teaches the *practice* of speaking with grace.

Together, they form a framework for leaders who want to communicate truth without losing compassion — leaders who want their words to reflect God's character as much as their actions do.

THE FRAMEWORK

This model rests on two anchoring passages of Scripture — one that defines the heart behind communication and one that shapes the way it is expressed.

1 Corinthians 13:4–8 establishes the posture of love.

It describes the inner disposition that must govern every conversation — patience over irritation, humility over pride, forgiveness over resentment. Love is not sentiment; it is disciplined strength under control. It determines how we approach correction, collaboration, and conflict. Before a leader speaks, love must shape the spirit in which the words are formed.

Ephesians 4:29 defines the practice of grace-filled speech.

It moves communication from attitude to action. Words are not to be careless or corrosive, but purposeful — building up, meeting the need of the moment, and extending grace to those who hear. If 1 Corinthians shapes the heart, Ephesians shapes the tongue.

Together, these passages create a balanced framework:

Love governs the motive.

Grace governs the method.

One addresses who we are becoming.

The other addresses how we speak.

In leadership, this pairing is essential. Truth without love becomes harsh. Love without truth becomes weak. But when love anchors the heart and grace directs the words, communication becomes redemptive — strengthening people while upholding standards.

This is the framework for leaders who desire their words to reflect God's character as clearly as their actions do.

THE FOUNDATION OF LOVE

1 Corinthians 13:4–8

LOVE IS PATIENT, LOVE IS KIND, IT IS NOT JEALOUS;
LOVE DOES NOT BRAG, IT IS NOT ARROGANT.

IT DOES NOT ACT DISGRACEFULLY, IT DOES NOT SEEK ITS OWN BENEFIT, IT IS NOT PROVOKED, IT DOES NOT KEEP AN ACCOUNT OF A WRONG SUFFERED.

IT DOES NOT REJOICE IN UNRIGHTEOUSNESS, BUT REJOICES WITH THE TRUTH; IT KEEPS EVERY CONFIDENCE, IT BELIEVES ALL THINGS, HOPES ALL THINGS, ENDURES ALL THINGS.

LOVE NEVER FAILS.

Love defines the posture of godly communication.

It is the attitude that turns correction into compassion and feedback into growth.

Without love, even truth can wound.

With love, truth becomes healing.

Love is not weakness—it is strength under control. It's what transforms leadership from authority into influence. It makes words life-giving instead of sharp, and gives the courage to speak truth without pride or fear. When love leads the heart, grace leads the tongue.

Love in Action:
Sixteen Markers of Grace-Driven Communication

These sixteen expressions of love provide a leadership checklist for grace-filled communication. They are not just traits to admire, but disciplines to practice in every meeting, message, and conversation.

1. Love is Patient
Endures frustration or disagreement without reacting harshly; it listens before speaking.

2. Love is Kind
Responds with gentleness and compassion, even when correction is needed.

3. Love is Not Jealous
Celebrates the success of others instead of competing with it.

4. Love Does Not Brag
Leads with humility; lets results speak instead of self-promotion.

5. Love is Not Arrogant
Values every person equally; refuses to use position or power for pride.

6. Love Does Not Act Disgracefully
Behaves honorably in all situations; guards speech and conduct from disrespect.

7. Love Does Not Seek Its Own Benefit
Prioritizes the team's good over personal convenience or recognition.

8. Love is not provoked

Maintains composure under pressure; does not respond defensively to criticism.

9. Love keeps no record of wrongs

Forgives quickly; releases grudges that poison communication.

10. Love does not rejoice in unrighteousness

Refuses to take pleasure in gossip, failure, or the humiliation of others.

11. Love rejoices with the truth

Stands for honesty, transparency, and integrity—even when truth is uncomfortable.

12. Love keeps every confidence

Protects others' dignity; keeps private matters private.

13. Love believes all things

Chooses to trust rather than assume the worst; gives people the benefit of the doubt.

14. Love hopes all things

Looks forward with optimism and faith, believing change and growth are possible.

15. Love endures all things

Perseveres through conflict, fatigue, or misunderstanding without quitting on people.

16. Love never fails

Remains constant even when results disappoint; love is the one leadership quality that never expires.

When these traits shape the way we communicate, leadership becomes more than management—it becomes ministry. Love refines tone, timing, and motive. It replaces frustration with patience, pride with humility, and reaction with grace.

Love does not ignore truth; it delivers it with compassion.
It does not avoid accountability; it brings it with care.
This is the foundation upon which every other principle rests.

BUILD IT WITH LOVE

Use this section to plan how you will start leading, building and comunicating in Love.

Build with Patience

> IN MY LEADERSHIP, WHERE DO I REACT TOO QUICKLY INSTEAD OF LISTENING?

____

____

____

> WHAT TEAM SITUATION CURRENTLY REQUIRES MORE PATIENCE FROM ME?

____

____

> HOW CAN I SLOW DOWN AND RESPOND MORE THOUGHTFULLY IN CONVERSATIONS?

____

____

____

> ONE CONVERSATION THIS WEEK WHERE I WILL CHOOSE PATIENCE:

____

____

Build with Kindness

> Does my tone make people feel valued or pressured? How?

> How can I correct someone while still encouraging them?

> Who on my team needs a more compassionate approach from me? Write something you could do differently.

Build without Jealousy

> Do I ever feel threatened by others' success or recognition? How?

> How does that affect the way I speak or lead?

> What is one way I can intentionally affirm someone this week?

Build without Bragging

> Do I highlight my achievements more than the team's effort? How?

____

____

____

> Where might I be seeking recognition in subtle ways?

____

____

____

> How can I shift the focus toward results and people instead of myself?

____

____

____

Build without Arrogance

> Do I listen as much as I speak in leadership conversations? How?

____

____

____

> Where might I be relying too much on my position or authority?

____

____

____

> How can I show value to others regardless of their role?

____

____

____

____

Build with Honor

(Love does not act disgracefully)

> ARE THERE MOMENTS WHERE MY TONE OR BEHAVIOR LACKS RESPECT?

> WHAT SITUATIONS TEND TO BRING OUT CARELESS OR SHARP RESPONSES IN ME?

> WHAT WOULD A MORE HONORABLE AND RESPECTFUL RESPONSE LOOK LIKE?

Build for Others, Not Self

(Love does not seek its own benefit)

> DO I PRIORITIZE MY CONVENIENCE OVER WHAT OTHERS NEED?

> WHERE MIGHT SELF-INTEREST BE SHAPING MY DECISIONS OR COMMUNICATION?

> WHAT IS ONE WAY I CAN SERVE SOMEONE ON MY TEAM THIS WEEK?

Build with Self-Control

(Love is not provoked)

> WHAT KIND OF FEEDBACK OR SITUATIONS TRIGGER ME EMOTIONALLY?

> HOW DO I USUALLY RESPOND WHEN CHALLENGED OR CORRECTED?

> WHAT WOULD A CALM, CONTROLLED RESPONSE LOOK LIKE IN THOSE MOMENTS?

Build with Forgiveness

(Love keeps no record of wrongs)

> AM I HOLDING ONTO PAST MISTAKES OR FRUSTRATIONS WITH SOMEONE?

> HOW IS THAT AFFECTING MY COMMUNICATION WITH THEM?

> WHAT WOULD IT LOOK LIKE TO RELEASE THAT AND MOVE FORWARD?

Build with Integrity

(Love does not rejoice in unrighteousness)

> Do I ever allow or participate in unhealthy conversations (gossip, criticism)?

> What kind of communication culture am I creating around me?

> How can I redirect conversations toward what is right and helpful?

Build with Truth

(Love rejoices with the truth)

> Do I avoid difficult truths to keep things comfortable?

> Where do I need to communicate more clearly or honestly?

> How can I speak truth in a way that builds rather than harms?

Build with Trust
(Love keeps every confidence)

> AM I TRUSTWORTHY WITH SENSITIVE OR PERSONAL INFORMATION?

> HAVE I EVER SHARED SOMETHING I SHOULD HAVE PROTECTED?

How can I strengthen trust through my communication?

Build with Confidence in Others
(Love believes all things)

> DO I TEND TO ASSUME THE WORST ABOUT OTHERS' INTENTIONS?

> IN WHAT SITUATIONS DO I BECOME CRITICAL OR SUSPICIOUS?

> HOW CAN I GIVE OTHERS THE BENEFIT OF THE DOUBT MORE CONSISTENTLY?

Build with Hope

(Love hopes all things)

> DO MY WORDS INSPIRE GROWTH OR REINFORCE DISCOURAGEMENT?

> WHERE HAVE I STOPPED BELIEVING IN SOMEONE'S POTENTIAL?

> HOW CAN I COMMUNICATE HOPE AND POSSIBILITY THIS WEEK?

Build with Perseverance

(Love endures all things)

> WHERE AM I TEMPTED TO GIVE UP ON A PERSON OR SITUATION?

> WHAT MAKES PERSEVERANCE DIFFICULT FOR ME IN LEADERSHIP?

> WHAT WOULD IT LOOK LIKE TO STAY COMMITTED AND ENGAGED?

Build with Consistent Love

(Love never fails)

> Is my leadership consistent, or does it depend on results or mood?

____

____

____

> When do I tend to withdraw or disengage from others?

____

____

____

> What would it look like to lead with steady, dependable care?

____

____

____

THE PRACTICE OF GRACE

Ephesians 4:29

LET NO UNWHOLESOME WORD COME OUT OF YOUR MOUTH, BUT IF THERE IS ANY GOOD WORD FOR EDIFICATION ACCORDING TO THE NEED OF THE MOMENT, SAY THAT, SO THAT IT WILL GIVE GRACE TO THOSE WHO HEAR.

While 1 Corinthians 13 defines **the posture** of communication, Ephesians 4:29 describes **the practice** — how love actually sounds when it speaks.

This verse is both simple and profound. It does not merely instruct believers to "avoid bad words"; it calls us to use speech with purpose. Every sentence becomes a tool — to *build up*, to *encourage*, to *guide*, to *heal*.

Grace-filled communication is intentional. It asks:

- "Will this strengthen or weaken the person listening?"
- "Is this what they need to hear right now?"
- "Does it reflect the kindness and truth of God?"

Paul's words invite us to a higher standard: to speak not reactively, but redemptively — using language that shapes hearts, restores trust, and advances God's purposes in every environment, including the workplace.

The Language of Grace:
Key Words that Transform Communication

Each key word in Ephesians 4:29 carries rich meaning and offers a lens through which to evaluate our speech. Understanding them deepens how we lead, correct, and encourage others.

1. Unwholesome (Greek: sapros)

Literally "rotten" or "decaying." It refers to words that damage rather than build — speech that spreads negativity, criticism, or cynicism.

Leadership principle: Avoid words that corrupt trust or morale. Healthy communication nourishes the environment around it.

2. Word (Greek: logos)

Means "spoken or written expression," but also "message" or "reason."

Leadership principle: Words reveal intent. Speak purposefully, with thought and reason, not just emotion.

3. Edification (Greek: oikodomē)

Means "to build up, strengthen, or promote growth," like constructing a building.

Leadership principle: Speak in ways that add value — affirm effort, clarify vision, and develop potential in others.

4. Need of the Moment (Greek: kata chreian)

Means "according to what is necessary" — speech that fits the situation or timing.

Leadership principle: Wisdom is not just knowing what to say, but *when* and *how* to say it. Tailor your words to meet the emotional and practical needs of the moment.

5. Grace (Greek: charis)

Means "favor, kindness, or divine influence on the heart."

Leadership principle: Let every word reflect undeserved kindness. Even correction can communicate grace when spoken with the goal of redemption, not punishment.

6. Hear (Greek: akouō)

Means "to listen, understand, or pay attention."

Leadership principle: Speak for the listener's benefit, not your own release. The goal of godly communication is not to be heard, but to be *understood*.

Grace-filled communication balances **truth and tenderness.** It confronts without condemnation and corrects without crushing. It meets the need of the moment — not by saying what's easiest, but by saying what's *most edifying*.

When our words reflect this verse, they do more than solve problems; they shape people. They carry the echo of God's grace into every conversation, transforming work environments into places where honesty, accountability, and kindness coexist.

BUILD IT WITH GRACE

Use this section to plan how you will start leading, building and comunicating in Grace.

Build without Unwholesome Words

(Avoid speech that damages trust or morale)

> WHAT KIND OF WORDS OR TONES TEND TO BRING NEGATIVITY INTO MY COMMUNICATION?

___

___

> WHEN AM I MOST LIKELY TO SPEAK IN A WAY THAT DISCOURAGES OTHERS?

___

___

> WHAT WOULD A HEALTHIER, MORE CONSTRUCTIVE RESPONSE SOUND LIKE?

___

___

Build with Purposeful Words

(Word – communication that carries intention and meaning)

> DO I SPEAK REACTIVELY, OR DO I THINK BEFORE I SPEAK?

___

___

> WHAT IS USUALLY DRIVING MY WORDS—EMOTION OR INTENTION?

___

___

> HOW CAN I COMMUNICATE MORE CLEARLY AND PURPOSEFULLY IN MY LEADERSHIP?

___

___

Build to Edify
(Speak in a way that builds others up)

> Do my words strengthen or weaken the people around me?

____
____
____

> Who on my team needs encouragement or affirmation right now?

____
____
____

> What is one way I can intentionally build someone up this week?

____
____
____

Build for the Moment
(According to the need of the moment)

> Do I consider timing and emotional context before speaking?

____
____
____

> What does this person truly need to hear right now?

____
____
____

> How can I adjust my tone and message to meet that need?

____
____
____

Build with Grace

(Speak with kindness that shapes the heart)

> Does my communication reflect kindness, even in correction?

> Where might I be too harsh or too direct without care?

> How can I communicate truth in a way that restores rather than discourages?

Build for the Listener

(Hear – communication aimed at being understood)

> Do I speak to express myself, or to truly help others understand?

> Do I take time to listen before responding?

> How can I communicate in a way that benefits the person listening?

THE MODEL IN MOTION

In the bustling offices of a multinational corporation, *James* served as a mid-level manager known for his calm presence and the unity within his team. His success was not driven by authority or charisma, but by a simple, consistent framework he carried into every conversation — one grounded in *love* and *grace*.

James often said that **1 Corinthians 13:4–8** reminded him *how* to feel toward others, and **Ephesians 4:29** reminded him *how* to speak to them. These verses had become his compass in leadership, shaping not just what he said, but the spirit behind it.

One day, a major project hit a crisis point. A team member, *Sarah*, made a costly mistake that resulted in a significant financial loss. The tension in the office was palpable. Many expected James to react with frustration or to make an example of her. But instead, he paused — and prayed for wisdom.

When he called Sarah into his office, his words reflected the grace he had learned to practice. He began not with accusation, but with empathy.

"We've all made mistakes," he said gently. "Let's walk through this together and see what we can learn."

He listened patiently as Sarah explained what had happened. Then, with both honesty and kindness, he addressed the issue directly, helping her identify the oversight and plan a way forward. Instead of leaving humiliated, Sarah left *restored* — determined to grow from the experience rather than hide from it.

Over time, this approach transformed James's team. People became more open, creative, and responsible because they felt safe to admit failure and learn from it. Accountability didn't disappear — it became stronger, rooted in mutual trust and respect.

James's leadership reflected what Scripture describes as *"speaking the truth in love"* (Ephesians 4:15). His communication was both honest and redemptive — never excusing mistakes, but always aiming to build character.

REFLECTION:

This story illustrates that accountability and compassion are not opposites; they are companions. When spoken with grace, correction strengthens rather than shames. Love does not ignore the truth — it delivers it with patience, timing, and care.

Grace-filled communication does more than manage relationships; it *heals* them. It restores confidence, rebuilds trust, and models the very character of Christ in the workplace.

LEADERSHIP TAKEAWAYS

Grace-filled communication is not a skill we master once—it's a discipline we practice daily. These takeaways summarize how love and grace shape leadership in every conversation.

Lead with Love Before You Speak Truth.

Truth without love hardens hearts; love without truth weakens character. Speak both with balance, so correction becomes care and honesty becomes healing.

Correct to Build, Not to Break.

The goal of accountability is growth, not humiliation. Every conversation should leave a person clearer, stronger, and closer to their God-given potential.

Seek Understanding Before Resolution.

Listening first communicates value. Often, what people need most is not an answer but to be heard and understood.

Be Intentional with Timing and Tone.

Even the right message can cause harm if delivered harshly or at the wrong moment. Grace waits for the right time and chooses the right tone.

Let Your Words Echo Your Faith.

Every sentence can be a reflection of God's heart. Speak as one who represents Him, offering words that bring clarity, peace, and encouragement wherever you go.

Communication is where faith becomes visible.

It's the meeting place between what we believe and how we treat people. Each word we speak carries the potential to build faith, restore trust, and reflect God's character.

When love defines your heart and grace guides your speech, even difficult conversations can become sacred moments of growth.

Your leadership will be remembered not only for what you accomplished but for how you made people feel—seen, valued, and encouraged to rise higher.

May your words always build, your tone always heal, and your leadership always point others back to Him.

Made in the USA
Monee, IL
04 November 2026

67386693R00115